Hidden Harbours of Wales

Published by
Imray Laurie Norie & Wilson Ltd
Wych House St Ives
Cambridgeshire PE27 5BT England
✆ +44 (0)1480 462114
Fax +44 (0)1480 496109
Email ilnw@imray.com
www.imray.com
2011

978 184623 373 9

British Library Cataloguing in Publication Data.
A catalogue record for this title is available from the British Library.

Printed in Singapore by Star Standard Industries Pte

Hidden Harbours

OF WALES

Dag Pike

Imray Laurie Norie & Wilson

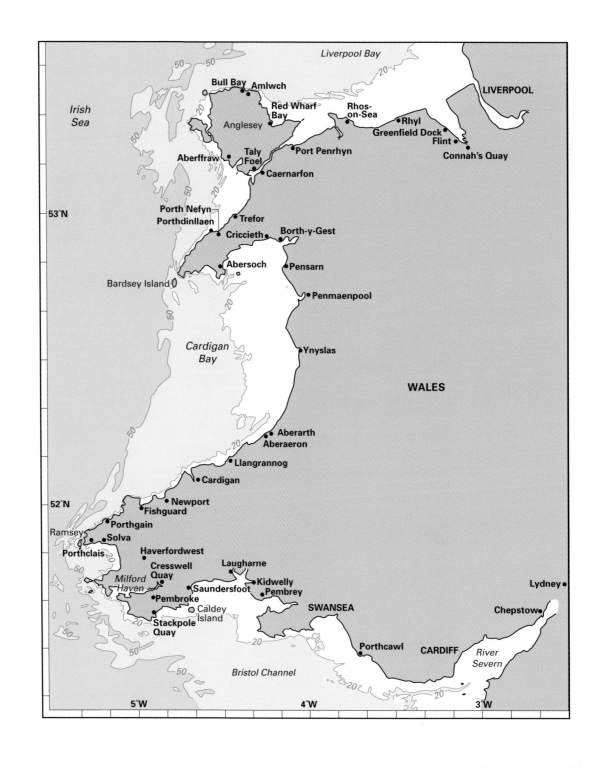

Liverpool Bay

LIVERPOOL

Irish
Sea

Bull Bay ● ● Amlwch
Red Wharf
Bay
Anglesey ● Rhos-
on-Sea
● Rhyl
Greenfield Dock
● Flint
Connah's Quay

Taly
Foel
Aberffraw ● ● Port Penrhyn
● Caernarfon

53°N

Porth Nefyn ● ● Trefor
Porthdinllaen
● Criccieth ● Borth-y-Gest

● Abersoch ● Pensarn

Bardsey Island ○
● Penmaenpool

● Ynyslas

Cardigan
Bay

WALES

● Aberarth
● Aberaeron

● Llangrannog

● Cardigan

52°N ● Newport
● Fishguard

● Porthgain
Ramsey ○
● Solva
Porthclais ● Haverfordwest
Cresswell ● Laugharne
Quay
Milford ● Saundersfoot ● Kidwelly
Haven ● Pembroke ● Pembrey
Caldey ○ SWANSEA
Island
Stackpole
Quay

● Lydney

● Chepstow

● Porthcawl CARDIFF River
Severn

Bristol Channel

5°W   4°W   3°W

Contents

Introduction

For seamen the Welsh coastline is a challenging place. Along the south coast bordering the Bristol Channel there are the strong tides and large tidal range to contend with. Along the west-facing coastline it is fully exposed to the prevailing westerly winds, so shelter is at a premium and for sailing ships there is the strong risk of getting 'embayed' on a lee shore. The north coast is a bit more sheltered and less demanding but here there are fewer sheltered coves and harbours available. When you look at the challenges that faced the captains of sailing ships trying to maintain trade around this coastline, it is not surprising to find that the rate of attrition was high and the list of casualties very long. This was bad news for the sailors but good news for the shipyards – and many of the ports along the Welsh coast had busy shipyards to meet the high demand for ships to replace those lost.

In view of the challenging conditions for seamen and the lack of suitable natural harbours (except for Milford Haven), you may wonder why there was much sea trade at all. However, Wales is rich in minerals: coal in the north and the south, slate in the north and also hard stone for building and limestone for agriculture, copper on Anglesey, and iron ore in both the north and the south. Where there are these abundant sources of minerals there will always be trade. With much of Wales being very mountainous and making overland travel difficult, trade by sea was the only solution; and when there is the potential for profit, the hazards of sea transport will always be worth the risk.

The mountains of Wales and the difficulties of land connections between West Wales and the rest of mainland Britain meant that sea trade was the only solution. Even when the railways came the main

The Welsh coastline can be a challenging place for seamen

tracks only ran along the north and south coastlines, so sea trade continued from ports around the wide sweep of Cardigan Bay long after rail transport had forced the closure or loss of trade at many of the southern and northern ports.

Then there was the fishing industry. In the Middle Ages the Irish Sea was teeming with herring and most of the ports around Cardigan Bay had a very active fishing fleet, so cargoes of salt were brought in to preserve the herring and cargoes of fish went out.

Cardigan Bay must have been the supreme challenge for seamen. Not only did it present a lee shore in the prevailing westerly winds but to the north and the south it was enclosed by projecting headlands. For a sailing ship that would struggle to head anything less than 90° in relation to the wind, this meant that escape would have proved difficult. Even when the wind was more favourable there was the long string of islands and rocks heading for 20 miles out to the Smalls Lighthouse to the south and the strong tides and unrelenting coastline of the Lleyn Peninsula to the north.

To the south the choice would have been to make passage between the rocks and islands then run out to the Smalls, but the tides here can run at up to 10 knots through the innermost passages of Jack and Ramsey Sounds. Further out there is the notorious Wild Goose Race that was a threat to any sailing ship and so the captains would be forced to take the long route out around the Smalls Lighthouse, doubling the length of the passage in many cases.

History suggests that quite a lot of the trade to and from Welsh harbours was across the Irish Sea. Coal was a major cargo on this trading route, which was mainly from South Wales; agricultural produce was a two-way trade, and limestone was also transported from the Welsh quarries for burning in the lime kilns in Ireland. Preserved fish and slate were also important cargoes.

Many small harbours were created to exploit the minerals of Wales

Then there were the harbours themselves. Many of them were located at the entrance to the rivers that swept down from the mountains inland. River entrances facing up to westerly gales would usually have shallow water across the entrance which combined with shifting sands to create a real hazard to ships trying to enter under sail. It would be a huge commitment on the part of the captain to take his ship into such a maze of shifting sands, knowing that there was no turning back once the entrance was attempted. We will never know just how many ships foundered in these harbour entrances just when they were on the verge of safety.

There was a considerable shipbuilding industry along the Welsh coast and this possibly reflects the high rate of attrition among the sailing ships that traded along this coastline. Virtually every port is recorded as having at least one shipyard and in

Many Welsh rivers end in extensive and dangerous estuaries

many of them there were several. These were small yards, perhaps building just two or three ships every year. One of the big advantages of these yards was the ready availability of the raw material for building wooden ships. There were forests around much of the coast in very close proximity to the yards and in those days the shipwrights would cut the timber that they needed for building the ships directly from the forests.

In addition to trading ships, these shipyards also built vessels for the fishing industry, which was very buoyant until the fish started to decline in the 1930s. Fishing was a major activity from the Welsh ports and with the relative inaccessibility of many of the Welsh ports to the markets inland, fish was exported to Ireland and Liverpool and down to the south.

It was the very dangers and relative inaccessibility of the small harbours around Cardigan Bay that made them attractive to smugglers. History suggests that smuggling was a major industry along this inhospitable coastline and, no doubt, the remoteness from the authority of the main population centres helped with this illicit trade. The high rewards from smuggling meant that the smugglers were more likely to take their chances with the vagaries of the weather and the challenging conditions.

Some of the harbours around Cardigan Bay were little more than open beaches where the ships would take ground as the tide receded and be unloaded by horse and cart. Remember that this was at a time when weather forecasts were not available. It was up to a captain to make his own forecast based on what he could see around him, a skill that is now largely lost as we rely on the radio and TV for forecasts. It is easy to see how road and rail transport quickly became the preferred option when these became available, and many of the harbours lost business. Many of the closures were accentuated by the silting of harbour entrances and even when steam took over from sail to make navigation more feasible under difficult conditions, Cardigan Bay was always a place feared by seamen.

Compared with the dangers of the western coastlines, the small harbours on the long tentacles of the Milford Haven estuary must have seemed like heaven to seamen. Here were water routes stretching way inland that were used for both import and export trade. The wide and safe entrance to the Haven gave easy and safe access to the open seas but unfortunately Milford Haven is not located near any major mineral resources. It has been left to the oil and gas industry to make use of this fine natural harbour in much more recent times, but even before this industry developed trade was already moving from the small inland ports to the deep-water quays downstream where larger ships could get access.

Along the Bristol Channel coastline the ports were the closest to the coalfields of South Wales and they became the major export route, so we now find only a few small ports here – and they have declined rapidly with silting as business moved to the larger ports. Some small ports that served local coal mines remain, and are covered in this book.

In the north it was slate that was king. This was exported to destinations around the globe but most of the ports serving the slate quarries were relatively small, so coastal shipping might take the slate to a major port such as Liverpool for trans-shipment. So much of the trade from the small ports of North Wales was with Liverpool that the two are inextricably linked. This applies to both cargo and passenger trades, with the beaches on North Wales providing any escape from the industrial cities of the north of England.

The Romans sailed their ships in the waters of Wales, with Chester being one of the major Roman ports. It was only the fishing and the lure of trade in various minerals that opened up many of the small ports to trade. Today there is very little in the way of trading shipping using the small ports of Wales and even some of the major ports such as Cardiff and Swansea are struggling as cheaper coal can be imported from abroad. Fishing was a mainstay of many of the smaller ports but commercial fishing has now also declined, to be replaced in many cases by the demand for sea angling. Today it is the leisure sector that is the main focus of many of the hidden harbours of Wales, with inshore fishing still maintaining a hold – and so life continues at these hidden harbours.

Some Welsh harbours were in remote locations

Mud is a feature of many harbours along the north sand south coasts of Wales

Lydney

Lydney Dock was built to handle the export of firstly iron ore and later coal from the Forest of Dean mines and it comprises both a canal and a dock area, with the entrance to the Severn Estuary through lock gates.

In the Middle Ages it was the last port on the River Severn where sea-going ships could dock until the Sharpness Canal was opened on the other side of the estuary, and with the ready supply of timber from the Forest of Dean it was also a shipbuilding centre.

The original port was developed on Lydney Pill, where the River Lyd flows into the estuary, and there was a wooden wharf constructed near the entrance to the Pill. However, the river was silting up and became unsuitable for moving cargoes by barge so Pidcock's Canal was built to bypass the shallow area. Work on the canal started in 1811 and this one-mile-long canal was opened two years later. It was connected to the coalfields by a tramway that operated with horse-drawn vehicles; later the horses were replaced by steam engines and the tramway was converted into a standard gauge railway. The increase in trade meant that the old wooden wharves became unsuitable and in 1809 work was started on building a new dock at the entrance. This new dock, the present-day Lydney Dock, was completed in 1821, eight years after the canal was opened, and trade through the port boomed. At its busiest time the port handled over 2,000 ships a year, with around 300,000 tons of cargo passing through the port. The port was originally designed to handle sailing ships but it made the transition to steamships around the turn of the 20th century and continued in use for cargoes right through to the 1970s, the main cargoes in later years being logs for processing at the local plywood factory.

The harbour was finally closed in 1977 and the decline started, but since 2003 a restoration project has been underway to recreate this working port. The restoration has entailed renewing the lock gates and their mechanisms, dredging out the basins and

The complex of locks and basins that form the entrance to Lydney Dock

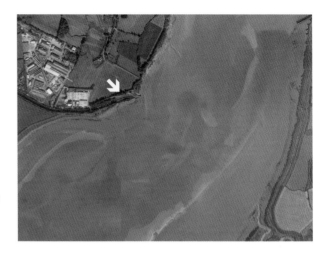

re-facing all the stonework as well as incorporating new flood defences. Despite all this restoration work you can still get a great impression of what Lydney Dock was like in its heyday.

Access by road

Lydney lies on the main A48 road on the north side of the Severn Estuary. To reach Lydney Dock you need to take the bypass and then watch for the turning on the roundabout that is signposted to Lydney Dock. Postcode for SatNav is GL15 4ER.

Parking

There is limited parking at the end of the lane that leads to the lock area.

Water access

To reach Lydney you first have to negotiate the tricky channels of the Severn Estuary. The approach to the lock entrance is straightforward but there are cross-tides even at high water when entry can be made. Contact the harbourmaster before arrival. There is berthing in the dock and permanent moorings in the canal above the dock.

The old canal basin above the locks that is now a peaceful mooring

The Victorian light at the entrance to Lydney Dock with Sharpness in the background

Facilities

The yacht club welcomes visitors but otherwise the nearest facilities are 1½ miles away in Lydney village.

More information

www.lydney-online.co.uk
Lydney Yacht Club www.lydneyyachtclub.co.uk
Harbourmaster ✆ 01684 864388

Comments

Today Lydney Dock is used by leisure craft, with many permanent moorings in the old canal section above the lock gates, but only a small section of the canal has been restored. There is an active yacht club in the old lock buildings and the restoration work has allowed this classified 'ancient monument' to give visitors an insight into what a 19th-century dock was like. Well worth a visit – even though it is not in Wales.

Chepstow

Chepstow was a port in Roman times and it is thought that there was a bridge across the river then, although further upstream than the existing bridge. It was the Normans who built the magnificent castle at Chepstow and the town grew up alongside the castle, with the port supplying much of its needs.

The port was the largest in Wales for many years and the records show that in the late 18th century it handled more cargo than Swansea, Cardiff and Newport put together. One of the reasons for this was that Chepstow's location made it an ideal place to transship cargoes. The deep water allowed shipping to enter and cargoes would be transshipped into barges to be taken up the River Wye or the River Severn, so Chepstow served a huge inland area. In the same way export cargoes came from the large hinterland of these rivers, timber being one of the main cargoes. Upriver very high quality paper was produced for the printing of banknotes; bark for tanning was another export. The ready availability of timber led to the establishment of a shipbuilding industry, so much of the trade – which went as far afield as Iceland and Turkey – was carried in locally built ships.

In the 19th century the importance of Chepstow as a port declined; the ports further west could handle larger ships, but the shipbuilding continued and in the First World War the first prefabricated ships were built on the slipways constructed on the river bank to the south of Chepstow. The ironwork for the Wye railway bridge had been built here and the Second World War saw the expansion of this shipyard to meet the demand for shipping. The yard could handle ships of up to 10,000 tons, but as the demand for ships of larger sizes grew the yard switched to building steel structures for bridges and other maritime structures such as lock gates. Fairfield Mabey Bridge (the company that built this steelwork) built the sections for the Severn Bridge at Chepstow and they were then floated out for erection. By a strange quirk of fate, one of the Aust ferries that the bridge replaced still lies under the

Chepstow bypass bridge. The yard is still building steelwork for bridges and also has plans to expand into the building of the support structures for marine wind farms.

Part of the old shipyard is now a base for sand and gravel distribution. This material is dredged in the Bristol Channel and brought in for landing on the quay, making this the only regular cargo remaining at this once busy port, although steel structures are occasionally shipped out by barge.

Access by road

Chepstow lies on the main A48 South Wales road. Postcode for SatNav is NP16 5HH.

Parking

There are several car parks in the town but one of the best for the river is the one that serves the castle and which is just off the main road to the old bridge.

Water access

Access to the river is quite straightforward from the River Severn just before the Severn Bridge and leaving Chapel Rock light off Beachley Point to starboard. Mooring is very tidal and difficult but Chepstow Boat Club is very helpful and there is a landing stage available from about half tide onwards. The river virtually dries out at low water springs.

Facilities

All the facilities of a town.

More information

Chepstow Town Council www.chepstow.co.uk
Gloucester Harbour Trust ☎ 01453 811913
www.gloucesterharbourtrustees.org.uk
The contact for the boat club moorings is Christine Norman
Email christine@orchard-bungalow.fsnet.co.uk
☎ 01291 624897

Comments

There is an active boat club at Chepstow but the very strong current means that leisure boating is restricted and considerable care is needed. The riverside has been redeveloped to include a flood defence wall but it is nevertheless an attractive area to visit and you still get a considerable feeling of the history of the place.

The beautiful old road bridge at Chepstow that links England and Wales

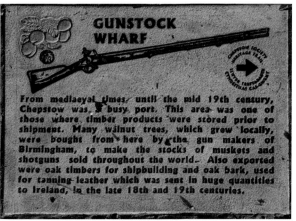

GUNSTOCK WHARF

From mediaeval times until the mid 19th century, Chepstow was a busy port. This area was one of those where timber products were stored prior to shipment. Many walnut trees, which grew locally, were bought from here by the gun makers of Birmingham, to make the stocks of muskets and shotguns sold throughout the world. Also exported were oak timbers for shipbuilding and oak bark, used for tanning leather which was sent in huge quantities to Ireland, in the late 18th and 19th centuries.

Plaque on the river bank that gives some of the history of Chepstow port

Porthcawl

The pier head lighthouse that marks the entrance to Porthcawl

Porthcawl is a relatively modern harbour in comparison to many Welsh harbours and it owes its creation and growth almost entirely to the requirement to export coal and iron ore. It is likely that there were fishing boats based at Porthcawl before the harbour was built, but these worked off the beach.

Work on the harbour started in the early 19th century with the aim of providing an export facility for the coal and iron ore mines located in the valleys north of Bridgend. The dock comprised an outer breakwater and the outer dock that can be seen today and the horse-drawn tramway that linked the port to the mines was opened in 1825. It took over six hours for one train to make the journey but despite this the port exported 35,000 tons of coal and 21,000 tons of iron ore in 1845. Warehouses were built on the quay in the outer harbour to house incoming cargoes; only one of these, the Jennings Building, survives today and is used as a skating centre.

In 1840 the docks were enlarged to cope with the expanding trade by adding a large inner basin on the north side which extended to 7.5 acres. This allowed larger ships to visit the port and was where much of the coal and iron ore was loaded into the ships from hoppers and chutes. To cope with this extra capability the tramway was upgraded to a full railway with steam engines and by 1871 the port was exporting 165,000 tons of coal. The outer entrance to the harbour was improved and at the same time gates were added to the inner basin so that it retained water to keep the ships afloat. This allowed larger ships to use the port and it remained competitive despite the competition from the then new ports at Port Talbot and Barry. Ten years later the port was in decline, largely due to the reduction in demand for iron ore, but trade picked up again with over 800 ships visiting the port in one year. However, the writing was on the wall as larger ships were used on the coal trade: by 1903 the tonnage had dwindled and in 1906 the inner harbour was closed. The remaining parts of the harbour started to make the transition to leisure requirements with the inner harbour becoming a boating lake. It was filled in during the Second World War but the entrance is still visible today.

The remaining parts of the harbour are used today by a large number of sea angling boats and leisure craft and a new lifeboat house has been built on the quay for the inshore lifeboat. The outer breakwater has been reinforced to cope with the battering of storms and the original cast iron lighthouse on the end of this breakwater is a feature.

Access by road

Porthcawl can be reached directly from Junction 37 of the M4. Take the A4229 which takes you right to the harbour. Postcode for SatNav is CF36 3YR.

Parking

There is limited road parking by the harbour and the filled-in section of the old inner harbour area is a pay car park for longer-term use.

Water access

Porthcawl is still a viable half-tide harbour and it is possible to moor alongside when there is no surge coming into the harbour. The local boats in the harbour lie to moorings because of this surge potential.

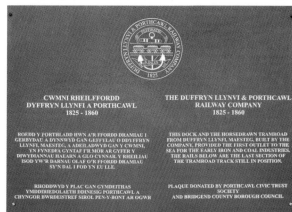

Facilities

All the facilities of a seaside tourist town.

More information

www.welcometoporthcawl.co.uk
Harbourmaster ☏ 01656 782756

Comments

Porthcawl is a seaside holiday town now, with
extensive caravan sites. The harbour is the one area
that retains some sense of history. There are plans
for expansion of the harbour again with the creation
of a large outer harbour that would be a marina
with lock gate access, but at present these are still on
paper.

*The basin at Porthcawl that
dries out at low water*

CWMNI RHEILFFORDD
DYFFRYN LLYNFI A PORTHCAWL
1825 - 1860

THE DUFFRYN LLYNVI & PORTHCAWL
RAILWAY COMPANY
1825 - 1860

*Historical plaque that details the
railway connections that brought
the cargoes to Porthcawl*

Pembrey

The South Wales coastline has a series of manmade harbours and docks that were almost all built to handle exports of coal from the prolific coalfield in the valleys and mountains. One of the earliest of them is Pembrey, located on the Burry Port or the River Loughor estuary. Despite facing almost due west and so being exposed to the prevailing winds, this estuary has deeper water at the entrance than the adjacent River Teifi estuary and so was more accessible to shipping.

Pembrey lies just inside the entrance to the estuary and the harbour was established by building a causeway out from the shore to provide berthing alongside the entrance channel to Pembrey Creek. This harbour was built in 1819 and was connected to the coalfields in the Grandraeth valley to the north by a network of canals and tramways to provide a safer and more convenient outlet for the coal trade. Prior to this development the small harbour area had been the base for a small fishing fleet, but today there are no boats operating in the deserted harbour which has now become a centre for birdwatching. There was an ordnance factory set up on the nearby sand burrows but this has now closed down and the whole area has been developed as a country park with walks and cycle tracks, so the harbour area (except, of course, the causeway) is reverting to its original natural state. The causeway has recently been restored and at the circular head

there are magnificent views across the estuary towards the Gower Peninsula. The restoration work has renewed much of the protective stonework but the remains of the old wooden jetties can still be seen sticking out of the sands alongside the causeway, although today it requires a lot of imagination to picture this quite remote location as being the scene of a busy coal port.

Pembrey's reign as a busy port did not last long because the harbour starting to silt up and the decline was hastened when the adjacent Burry Port

Right The remains of the piling that once supported the wooden jetties at Pembrey

Far right Looking back towards the land from the head of the causeway

The old stone walls around the head of the causeway that formed the anchor point for the jetties

Dock was opened just half a mile away. This dock provided the more reliable facilities for shipping, with an easy entrance from the main channel and the picturesque lighthouse marking its entrance. The canals and railways also connected to this dock so that trade soon moved along the coast; the mainline railway also passed very close. Burry Port is now a busy marina and Pembrey was finally abandoned as a port in 1878.

Access by road

From the main road through the town of Burry Port follow the signs to the marina but take the first right following a sign to Seascape. Follow the road past this caravan site and on to a parking area from where you walk to the causeway. Postcode for SatNav is SA16 0EJ.

Parking

There is a small free parking area where the road ends.

Water access

The water access is via a twisting channel from the main River Loughor channel and access is really only practical by tender on a rising tide.

Facilities

The village of Pembrey and the town of Burry Port have most facilities and there are boating requirements in the marina.

More information

Pembrey and Burry Port Town Council
www.pembreyburryport-tc.gov.uk

Comments

Pembrey harbour has now reverted to a wild a beautiful area and is worth a visit, if only for the stunning views across the estuary.

Kidwelly

The restored dock basin at Kidwelly

Kidwelly owes its origins to the Normans, who established a castle and garrison here in the 12th century. The River Gwendraeth ran alongside the castle and was, no doubt, used to bring in supplies. The town of Kidwelly developed around the castle and there are records of ships that traded with Bristol and even as far afield as France. Much of the maritime traffic was concerned with the wars that raged in the 11th and 12th centuries but in the 14th century the town expanded, with a bridge built across the river and quays on the river banks. Cargoes exported from the port (such as wool and hides) were mainly related to farming and cargoes coming in comprised wine, salt and iron. However, the location of Kidwelly on a river creek winding in from the main Towy Estuary created hazards for shipping and in the 16th century there was

considerable silting that restricted sea trade. The port went into decline, only to revive again when the shifting sands created a deeper channel, allowing access to shipping again. The revival was focussed on the expanding coal trade from the local mines and the banks of the river below the bridge are reported to have been lined with quays, coalyards and warehouses. Iron products were also exported to ports around Britain.

There are two Gwendraeth rivers, the one that Kidwelly stands on and one just to the south, and they join up in the estuary. In 1766 a three-mile-long canal was built to link the two rivers in order to provide a route for the transport of coal from the pits close to the southern river. Where this canal linked into the north river a dock was built, and it is this that forms the small port that remains today. The canal skirted round the western edge of the town and parts of it can still be seen, particularly close to the dock area where it has been partially restored. This dock became the focus of the coal trade from Kidwelly but shipyards were also established along the river banks, and around this time Kidwelly was a busy and bustling port.

However, the sands in the estuary were a still a constant problem and various schemes were

proposed to improve the situation, but none came to fruition. Another factor that led to the decline was the completion of a canal system that linked the coal mines to Burry Port where there was easier access for the larger ships, so some of the coal trade was lost from Kidwelly. The building of a fixed railway bridge just above the dock completed the demise of much of the port of Kidwelly; the dock continued to export coal up until about 1920 when it was finally closed and became a waste tip.

Access by road

Enter Kidwelly from the north or the south and follow signs to the railway station. Station Road leads across a level crossing by the station and then on to the restored quay area. Postcode for SatNav is SA17 4UH.

Parking

There is limited free parking in the restored quay area.

Water access

A visit by tender on a rising tide could be possible, but the channel is not marked. Mooring in the restored dock could be possible.

Facilities

It is about half a mile from the dock to the town where there are all the usual facilities.

More information

www.kidwelly.gov.uk
www.kidwellyhistory.co.uk

Comments

Today much of the dock and part of the canal have been restored to convert the area for leisure use, although this is restricted to land rather than water. The restoration of the docks does give a feel for the past, but the absence of any vessels reduces the illusion. There are hopes that the river might eventually be opened again for access by yachts.

Looking out over the tidal entrance channel

The restored dock basin the led into the canal linking the two rivers

Laugharne

Laugharne is mainly famous as the temporary home of the writer Dylan Thomas and The Boathouse where he wrote some of his works is a feature of the village. The Boathouse is located along the steep sides of the estuary close to where there was originally a quay. However, the main feature of Laugharne is its castle which dominates the harbour area and which was one of a series of defensive castles along the coasts of the Bristol Channel and Pembrokeshire.

The harbour was located at the foot of the castle and along the shore and was used mainly to import supplies such as coal and other commodities that could not be produced locally. Silting of the harbour reduced its importance and the harbour today is more of a creek that runs in from the Afon Taf, which in turn is a tributary of the River Teifi. There were coal mines on the other side of the main estuary and it is likely that there was trade across the estuary rather than out to sea.

This whole estuary is a maze of shifting sandbanks that are not easy to negotiate and which presented a hazard to shipping, but the establishment of a small harbour at Laugharne demonstrates how important access to the sea was for bringing in cargoes and exporting local produce when road transport was so poor. Roman traces have been found in Laugharne, which suggests that they used this as a port, or at least explored up these rivers and creeks. Pictures of Laugharne Castle about 150 years ago show that the water was right up to the castle, but today the water comes up the small creeks and it is only on a big spring tide that the water covers the marshes, suggesting that over the years there was considerable silting that reduced the importance of the port.

One of the main claims to fame of Laugharne (apart from Dylan Thomas) is that is was the centre of a major cockle industry. The sands of the estuary are a perfect site for cockles and harvesting these shellfish was the focus of much of the trade. There was a cockle processing factory in the village but today there is very little trace of the history of Laugharne as a port, with just the remnants of a small quay under the cliffs and, of course, the castle that dominates what was the harbour.

Access by road

From the main A40 turn left at St Clears onto the A4066 which passes through the village. Postcode for SatNav is SA23 4SY.

Parking

Limited parking along the waterfront.

Water access

The only realistic water access is by tender and you have to feel your way into the creeks on a flooding tide, with the castle offering a guide as to the main direction.

The track that leads out to Dylan Thomas's Boathouse

The tidal creek that runs up to Laugharne with the remains of the wharf in the background

Facilities

There is a pub, the Cross House, in the village, as well as a shop and a café.

More information

www.laugharne.co.uk

Comments

Some small leisure craft are moored in the creek as a reminder of the maritime associations of the place and there is still a haunting atmosphere that makes this a very attractive place to visit even without the Dylan Thomas connection.

Looking across the creek to Laugharne castle

Saundersfoot

Today Saundersfoot Harbour looks like the perfect small seaside harbour with colourful boats rocking at moorings, but it has a significant industrial history. Coal has been mined in the hinterland for centuries and this coal or anthracite is some of the cleanest to burn, burning with an intense heat which makes it ideal for smelting mineral ores.

Initially the coal from the small private pits was brought down to Saundersfoot by horse and cart and loaded into small ships that had been beached over the low water. Saundersfoot, facing east, is well sheltered from the westerly winds and so this beach loading could be carried out on the majority of days. The beach was also used by a number of fishing boats but, as demand for the high quality coal increased, so the demand for better facilities grew and the construction started on the harbour in 1828. Combined with this harbour development was the expansion of the mines into larger and deeper pits and the construction of a tramway from the pits to the harbour, so the cargoes exported from Saundersfoot expanded rapidly and iron ore was also exported in addition to coal. At first the trucks on the tramway were towed by horses but these were replaced by steam engines in 1870 to increase the capacity. The coal was brought in by small trucks and was dumped into hoppers on the quay, from where it could be loaded directly into the ships' holds. By this time many of the sailing ships had been replaced by steam ships and Saundersfoot was a busy industrial port operated by the Saundersfoot Railway and Harbour Company.

Because of the way in which the harbour was built under the cliffs and with the beach on its northern side where the entrance lay, it was prone to silting across the entrance. To counteract this, a sluicing basin was constructed across the west side of the harbour. Both the water from the rising tide and the water from the stream that ran into the harbour were captured in this basin and held there at high tide, then released at low water through sluice gates to create a flow of water to wash out the channel through the sand.

The dock basin at Saundersfoot viewed from the pier head

By the 1920s the coal industry was declining in Pembrokeshire; the cargoes exported from Saundersfoot followed suit and in the 1930s the coal trade ceased in the face of competition from the major South Wales ports and the coming of the railway. Fishing continued at the harbour and today Saundersfoot is a significant base for sea angling boats and a few commercial fishing boats. The sluicing basin still exists but is not used.

Access by road

Saundersfoot is well signposted from the main A478 and the harbour is found after driving through the village. Postcode for SatNav is SA69 9HE.

Parking

There is parking on the north pier and in a car park on the adjacent sea front.

The dock basin with the scoured channel from the river water

*The watch tower and light
on the pier head*

Water access

The harbour is available for two hours either side of high water and dries out completely at low water. The entrance channel runs well north of the east pier so pass about 100m off until the entrance opens and then keep close to the north pier. Mooring alongside is possible but space is limited.

Facilities

All the facilities of a small town, plus a boatyard and a chandlery.

More information

www.visit-saundersfoot.com
Harbourmaster ☎ 01834 812094

Comments

Saundersfoot still remains a very attractive harbour and is used by both yachts and fishing boats. Located at the southern end of the beach, it makes Saundersfoot the picture-postcard-perfect small seaside town and is well worth a visit.

Stackpole Quay

Harbours do not come much smaller than this: there is just room inside the harbour at Stackpole for a couple of fishing boats to moor up. The harbour lies on a tiny inlet from the sea on the east side of the southern Pembrokeshire peninsula near St Govan's Head there was a small quay established on this site in the 17th century to import small quantities of coal from the mines near Saundersfoot a few miles along to coast to the east. This coal was used with the limestone from nearby quarries to produce lime for the farms and it was this established feasibility of having a port in the inlet that encouraged the Earl of Cawdor to improve the harbour with the building of a stone breakwater. The Earl wanted a harbour from where he could ship out the valuable limestone from his nearby quarries and also a place where he could import luxury goods for use in his home at Stackpole Court.

The use of this harbour must have been opportunistic, because the breakwater does not offer full protection when there is a heavy swell running outside and when the wind in the east. The vulnerability of the harbour can be seen today in that the mooring ropes used to locate the fishing boats in the middle of the harbour and to cope with the surge are the size of the ropes used to moor super tankers.

The harbour, like the house, is now owned by the National Trust, which has invested heavily in rebuilding and refurbishing the quay wall so that it is in a fit state to withstand the winter gales. Not only has the quay wall been rebuilt but the entrance channel has been cleared, with a low retaining wall on the south side of the channel to contain the loose rocks that are outside the main quay wall and which serve to help break up the incoming waves. In addition to the small harbour located behind the quay wall, there is also a rough ramp at the head of the creek which can serve as a launching site for small fishing boats and tenders.

The narrow entrance channel with the rocks held back by a low rock wall

Stackpole Quay lies on a beautiful unspoilt coastline and is virtually the only harbour along a 20-mile stretch of exposed coast between Milford Haven to the west and Tenby to the east.

Access by road

Take the B4319 out of Pembroke. Turn left in Stackpole village and there is a sign pointing to the narrow road that leads to the quay. Postcode for SatNav is SA71 5LS.

Parking

The National Trust has quite a large, well signposted pay and display car park just inland from the quay.

Water access

You could come into Stackpole by tender after anchoring off. The entrance does not show up well until you are close but there are a couple of moorings off the entrance which the fishing boats use in good conditions.

Facilities

The National Trust runs a tea room, located between the car park and the inlet.

More information

www.nationaltrust.org.uk
Email stackpole@nationaltrust.org.uk
Estate office ✆ 01646 661359
Tea rooms ✆ 01646 672687

Comments

Stackpole Quay is the archetypal hidden harbour, tucked away amongst the rocks so that you almost come on it as a surprise. You stare in admiration at the ability to construct such a small harbour in such an unlikely place.

The tiny harbour at Stackpole Quay where there is just room for two boats

Pembroke

Pembroke, as distinct from Pembroke Dock, has a long maritime history, but it is turning its back on this heritage and many significant sites of marine activity are disappearing. The town lies on the Pembroke River that wanders in from Milford Haven and it is along this section of the river that an early graving dock and quarries are being filled in to allow modern building. There are some remains of medieval and Elizabethan shipbuilding slipways along the river banks but they are hard to find and are not featured. Pembroke expanded as a port when the main port of the area upriver at Haverfordwest declined, and for a long time Pembroke was the main port for passengers wanting to travel to Ireland. It is a long and twisting channel up to Pembroke but the attraction of the town was the spur of land at the point where the river divided and where the dominant castle now stands. The river on both sides of the castle formed the main harbour area, particularly on the south side where the last remaining corn store on the corner by the bridge

The Cornstore is the last remaining warehouse on the quay

provides a glimpse of the past. Historically the port at Pembroke dates back to Roman times but it was in the Middle Ages that it developed as a major port, with various charters giving the town control over all the goods entering the whole of Milford Haven. The port was still in use in the 19th century, with imports of coal, lime, bricks and timber, and the last trading vessel to use the port arrived in 1961. Exports comprised wool, hides, fish and farm produce, the main trade being to Ireland and France. Three factors led to the decline of Pembroke as a port and, as in so many harbours, one was the arrival of the railways. Then when the Royal Navy decided to build Pembroke Dock on the main estuary for building and servicing naval vessels, this also took trade from Pembroke; finally, the river was silting up, restricting access. More recently a barrage has been built across the river just downstream of the castle in order to maintain water levels around the castle area. This has restricted boat access to the harbour area but there is a lifting sluice that can allow access for small craft close to high water. The old bridge across the river also incorporated a tidal mill so that the water level above the bridge has always been controlled.

Access by road

Pembroke has well signposted access from the A477 and from the Neyland Bridge, but don't confuse it with Pembroke Dock which is a separate town. Postcode for SatNav is SA71 4NQ.

Parking

There is pay and display parking on the quays and the long term car park now covers the area where there were more quays on the south side of the castle.

Water access

It is a long and winding river access to Pembroke and these days it is more suited to exploration by tender. It is possible for smaller craft to gain access to the water above the barrage (given due notice) and to moor in the centre of town.

Facilities

All the facilities of a small town, including pubs and restaurants close by the quays.

More information

www.pembroketownguide.co.uk

Comments

It is difficult to picture the bustling activity of the once busy port and the harbour area is now almost sterile, with not a boat in sight. The tourism focus is on the castle and virtually all the maritime focus is now transferred to Pembroke Dock.

The quay wall sits beneath the imposing castle

The tidal river that leads out to the sea

Cresswell Quay

Cresswell Quay looks so far off the beaten track that you have to wonder how and why it was developed. There does not seem to be much to attract water trade to the area but then you discover that there were coal mines in nearby Reynalton, Loveston and Yerbeston, and with Cresswell Quay being the nearest point where the coal could be shipped out its reason for development becomes apparent.

This whole area was also a major source of limestone, so here you have the two ingredients that formed much of the cargo shipped into many of the small harbours around the Welsh coast. The whole area around the creek leading up to Cresswell Quay is riddled with limestone quarries and there were also similar small quays up many of the nearby creeks where the limestone was shipped out. Much of the limestone was also used for building work and the defensive forts and castles around Milford Haven are built mainly from this local material.

The coal exports from Cresswell Quay reached their peak in the 18th century, when there were three quays in use at the harbour together with an extensive coal storage yard. Due to the shallow water in the Cresswell River the coal was mainly shipped out from the quay in barges of around 20 tons and transshipped down river into seagoing vessels. Records from the late 18th century show that there were 10 of these barges associated with the trade. In the early 19th century the price of coal being exported from Cresswell Quay could not compete with the larger coal mines and export facilities along the south coast of Wales and the coal trade declined, but the quay was still used to bring in a variety of goods and to export farm produce and it continued in use into the 20th century. Today there is a triangular quay located at the junction of the main river and a small tributary and this is now mainly used as a picnic and sitting-out area for the pub across the road from the quay. Local yachts and tenders make their way up the twisting river for an evening cruise, with the pub as the focus of the voyage. On the river

above the quay there are stepping stones where the river can be crossed below about half tide and on the wall of the pub there is one of the original AA road signs.

Access by road
From the A477 main road to Pembroke take the A4075 northwards; the turning for Cresswell is seen on the left. Postcode for SatNav is SA68 0TE.

Parking
On the road by the pub and on the quay itself.

Water access
Local knowledge is needed to find the way up the twisting creek, but a visit by tender is very practical on a rising tide with the pub at the end to lure you on.

The vintage AA sign on the quay at Cresswell

AUTOMOBILE ASSOCIATION

PEMBROKE 7
CRESSWELL
HAVERFORDWEST 14
LONDON 237¼
SAFETY FIRST

Facilities

The Cresselly Arms is the only facility here. No food is served at the pub.

More information

Milford Haven Port Authority www.mhpa.co.uk
Good Pub Guide www.thegoodpubguide.co.uk

Comments

A popular spot on summer evenings, but there is very little left to show that is was a busy small coal quay except the quay itself which can still be used. Apart from the pub and the houses in the village this is quite wild and remote country.

The quay and steeping stones on a winter's day

Haverfordwest

A plaque on the restored building on the quay

You could not ask for a more central location for a port than Haverfordwest. It is right in the centre of the Pembrokeshire peninsula and even today, when the port has declined almost to the point of extinction, this town is still the centre of the region. In the past its location made Haverfordwest a major port for the region despite the long journey up the Milford Haven estuary to reach it.

There is evidence that the Romans used the river. It started as a port back in 900AD, when settlers from Scandinavia arrived at the head of the river, and by the 13th century it was a major port. Its importance can be judged by the fact that the mayor of the town is also known as the Admiral of the Port of Haverfordwest. Export cargoes came from the farmland around the town but also included coal from the small local mines, whilst imports included most of the goods not available locally, such as textiles, hardware, oil, tar and iron. The main quay was on the west side of the river where the deeper water lay and this street, now known as Quay Street but formally known as Ship Street, was full of ale houses, chandlers and warehouses. Haverfordwest was also home to some pirate ships in the Middle Ages and these seem to have been tolerated as long as they did not attack local shipping.

The castle sitting above the port indicated the importance of the place, but by 17th century the port was in decline, partly as a result of the civil wars and the plague, but also because the trading ships were getting larger and so finding it more difficult to navigate the long and winding route up the river. Silting also took place in the river and the plan to carry out major improvements to the port in the 19th century was never enacted because the railway came to Haverfordwest and took away much of the marine trade. Ships were still used to bring in bulk cargoes and Haverfordwest remained open to shipping right through till the 1930s when trading finally ceased.

Today it is as though the port facilities have been frozen in time with the quays and several of the old buildings still in place along Quay Street, but it has a sleepy atmosphere and the town seems to have turned its back on its maritime history.

Access by road

Avoid taking the bypass around the town and head south towards Milford Haven when the quays will be seen on the left after crossing the river. Postcode for SatNav is SA61 1BB.

Parking

There is parking along Quay Street but it is very busy and more road parking can usually be found along towards the Priory ruins.

Water access

The channel up the Western Cleddau is well marked in the early stages but then it is mainly a question of staying in the centre of the channel. There is limited headroom under the bridges as you approach the town. It is possible to tie up alongside the quay but this is rough stone, so a visit to Haverfordwest might be best by tender.

Facilities

All the facilities of a town are available close by and there is a pub on the quay itself.

More information

www.haverfordwesttown.co.uk

Comments

So-called 'improvements' along the river (such as the building of a weir across the river just upriver from the quays, and the construction of unsympathetic council offices on the opposite bank) have taken away some of the attraction of the place. It is still possible to travel upriver by boat and to tie up at the old quays, but the river at Haverfordwest is now just that and it is hard to imagine the hustle and bustle of the busy port of the past.

The old quay wall with the barrage and new council offices in the distance

Solva

Solva has rivalled nearby Porthclais as the main port for St Davids, but because it was further away it mainly functioned as a port to serve the extensive farmland of the St Davids Peninsula. With this in mind it became a major lime burning centre and there were 10 lime kilns in operation here during Victorian times. This meant that the main imports were coal and limestone. The remains of some of the lime kilns can be seen on the east side of the harbour close by the head of the inlet. Because the harbour has a bend in the inlet it is better protected from the sea outside than some of the smaller inlets along this coast, so there has not been the requirement to build a breakwater.

Solva has a long history: there are the remains of an Iron Age fort and Norsemen are reported to have used the harbour. In 1900 there were 30 ships registered at Solva and it was possible to sail directly to America from here on the emigrant ships. Farm produce was the main export, with timber and, of course, coal and limestone coming in. There were nine warehouses on the quay but one of the main features of the history of Solva is seen in the Trinity Quay, was built on the west side of the harbour about halfway up the inlet. This was built as the base for the construction of the Smalls Lighthouse that is situated on rocks some 20 miles out to seaward from Solva. It was here that the Cornish granite for the construction was brought in and it was then dressed and shaped on the quay before being shipped out to the construction site. Most of this construction work took place in the middle of the 19th century; this quay then formed the basis of the main trade quay where cargoes were brought in and exported.

There is an old lifeboat house on the quay with its launching slipway still in place, but this is no longer and active lifeboat station. Solva has always been a fishing port and today there are still a few active fishing boats operating from it but most of the activity in the harbour is leisure these days. The harbour has a mainly sandy bottom which is filled with an extensive array of moorings and the rocks

Plaque on the old lifeboat house

outside the entrance break up the waves and make this a good sheltered harbour.

Access by road

Access to the harbour is directly on the A487 coast road at the point where it makes a sharp turn up the hill. Postcode for SatNav is SA62 6UT.

Parking

There is a large car park right on the quay in front of the Ship Inn.

Water access

The entrance is well hidden until you are almost right up to it and is well disguised by the offlying rocks that shelter the entrance. Once inside, the main channel keeps to the west side with half-tide access to Trinity Quay where the Solva Boat Club is located. No anchorage is possible because of extensive moorings in the harbour.

Facilities

There are three pubs in Solva, plus cafés and shops. The Solva Boat Club welcomes visitors. Sail Sailboats offers repairs.

More information

Solva Harbourmaster
☎ 01437 721703 or 07974 020139
Solva Boat Owners Association ☎ 01437 721220

Comments

Solva is a very pretty harbour with a lot of history and it caters well for visitors, in terms of both facilities and access.

Trinity Quay that was built as a base for the building of the Smalls Lighthouse

Porthclais

Porthclais is an inlet from St Brides Bay that offers a degree of shelter from the prevailing winds. It was developed as a port in Roman times and it is thought that the old quay wall at the head of the inlet is still part of the original Roman construction.

The importance of Porthclais grew in the 12th century when it was the port for nearby St Davids and was used for the importing of much of the stone used to build the cathedral and the Bishop's Palace there. It was also used to import coal and limestone to create lime for the surrounding farms and the limekilns on the quay are reputed to be some of the best preserved in Pembrokeshire. Timber was also imported because there was not a lot of woodland on the exposed land in this part of Pembrokeshire.

The port expanded in importance and the quay was rebuilt in the Middle Ages. The quay at the head of the inlet is very tidal and the whole inlet was subject to considerable swells coming in from

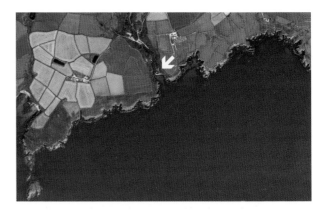

seaward, so the outer breakwater was built, originally from the stones and boulders that littered the harbour bed. This construction served to both clear the harbour and make it safer for boats and ships to dry out in, and to offer better protection.

The quay inside the harbour that was the original base in Roman times

The breakwater has since been rebuilt into a stronger and more permanent structure and it extends almost right across the entrance, leaving just a narrow channel on the west side as the entrance. There is a small quay on the west side (not far inside this entrance) that would be available at around half tide and which may have been used as an alternative landing place to the quay at the head of the inlet. As the roads improved the importance of Porthclais as a harbour diminished, although up to the beginning of the 20th century it was used for the two-way trade of coal, fertilisers, building materials and timber coming in and mainly farm produce going out.

Porthclais has always been a fishing port and this is its main commercial function today, although the harbour is mainly used for leisure craft and angling boats. The breakwater has not entirely eliminated the swells that can come into the harbour so that boats in the harbour are on moorings rather than lying alongside. At the head of the creek there is a slate slab bridge over the stream that is largely hidden by the more modern road bridge.

Access by road

From St Davids, Porthclais is signposted along a narrow single-track road. Postcode for SatNav is SA62 6RR.

The restored limekilns

The tiny outer breakwater and harbour with the narrow entrance channel

Parking

After crossing the bridge and turning right, there is a car park with a £2 charge.

Water access

The entrance is not easy to see until you are quite close but there are no offlying rocks so the entrance is easy; but keep to port to find the passage past the breakwater. Contact the harbourmaster for a mooring and avoid mooring on the inside of the breakwater because the wall has staggered steps underwater.

Facilities

This is National Trust property and there is a small café at the head of the inlet in the summer.

More information

Porthclais Harbourmaster
☏ 01437 720437 or 07974 044960

Comments

This is a beautiful small harbour, a true 'hidden harbour' that still retains a sense of history but has remained viable into the modern age.

Porthgain

Porthgain is a small inlet on the north coast of Pembrokeshire that has been developed into a more secure harbour by building breakwaters across the entrance.

Before the breakwaters were built it was used as a fishing harbour and then to bring in cargoes such as limestone and coal to make lime for spreading on the local fields. The lime kiln where the lime was made can still be seen in the harbour and is reputed to be the oldest building in the village. Porthgain developed as a more important harbour when slate was quarried at nearby sites and the harbour was developed to export it.

Since then the harbour has had three major periods of development relating to the cargoes being handled there. First it was the slate, which was brought down to the harbour by a tramway to a slate-cutting facility which was water powered by the stream that ran into the harbour. There was also a tunnel from the quarry to the harbour but this has been blocked off. The slate-cutting building still stands in the harbour, with part of it now used as a café. The slate export continued until around 1910. At the end of the 19th century it was discovered that the waste from the slate could be used for brick making and by the turn of the century up to 50,000 bricks a week were being made at Porthgain, mostly for export from the port. The brick factory was in the centre of the quay, with numerous outbuildings and at much the same time the port was used for the export of crushed road stone. The hoppers that held the crushed stone can still be seen on the west side of the harbour, constructed from locally made bricks. These were filled up from above so that the stone could be loaded directly into the ships from the hoppers under gravity. A narrow-gauge railway was laid into the village to bring in the raw materials for the brick making and the rock for the roadstone, and a stone crusher was erected above the hoppers. The brick making stopped around 1912 but Porthgain was a hive of industry up until about 1930, when the export of the roadstone also stopped

and the harbour reverted to its original use as a fishing harbour, with a small fleet now operating out of the port, as well as many leisure craft.

Today this north-facing harbour is well protected from the prevailing winds and the breakwaters give added protection.

Access by road

Porthgain is signposted off the main A487 coast road. Postcode for SatNav is SA62 5BN.

Parking

There is some parking on the quay and limited free parking around the village.

The entrance with the watch tower and the beacon in the distance

Water access

Porthgain can be indentified from seaward by the white daymarks on each side of the entrance. There are moorings in the harbour but short-term visitors can moor alongside the quay walls if there is no surge in the harbour.

Facilities

The historic Sloop Inn in the village is the centre of social life and there is a café/bistro in the old slate-cutting building on the quay.

More information

Pembrokeshire National Park
www.pcnpa.org.uk

Comments

At the back of the harbour there is a village green with houses around it, making this a very attractive place to visit. The relics of the industrial past tower above the harbour on the west side, taking away any picture-postcard appeal from the harbour, but this is still a very attractive harbour to visit.

The remains of the brick built hoppers used for storing and loading stone

The small harbour with the modern slipway

Fishguard

To many people Fishguard is hardly a 'hidden harbour' because it is the harbour from which they depart to Ireland. However, that is strictly speaking Goodwick, and Fishguard is the harbour on the small estuary of the River Gwaun tucked away on the other side of the bay. The name originates from a Nordic word meaning 'fish-catching enclosure' and Fishguard, or Lower Fishguard as it is more strictly called, has always been primarily a fishing harbour.

In the 18th century there was a large fishing fleet based here to exploit the Irish Sea herring and salted herring was one of the main exports travelling to British and Irish ports. Imports were mainly coal and limestone but it was fishing that was the backbone of trade. In 1797 Fishguard was the scene of what is thought to be the last invasion of Britain and it was here that the Battle of Fishguard was fought with the French. As the herring fishery declined so did the port, and the maritime focus of the area switched to the other side of the bay when it was decided to develop this as the terminus for the Irish packet boats.

The long breakwater of this new harbour extending out into the bay improved the level of shelter at Lower Fishguard to make the harbour more tenable in strong winds, but the harbour still declined and today the focus has switched mainly to leisure use. Several fishing boats still operate out of the harbour, using the outer end of the short quay wall extension as their base.

The harbour itself still retains a traditional look, with long, low houses converted from the warehouses that lined the long quay wall. This traditional look was exploited in 1972 when the harbour was used for the filming of Dylan Thomas's *Under Milk Wood*; *Moby Dick* was also partially filmed here. The River Gwaun that tumbles down from the hills meets the harbour area at the point where the main road bridge crosses the river. From here the harbour widens out into a good-sized bay, but much of this water area dries out over low water and with the swell that comes in from seaward these

moorings are not tenable for much of the year. The same applies to the long quay wall along the east side of the harbour where the main channel lies and all boats lie off at moorings.

There has been talk of developing a marina in the area to cater for the increase in yachting but this is likely to be in the Goodwick part of the harbour rather than in Fishguard itself.

Access by road

The main A487 coast road passes across the bridge at the top of the harbour and the quay is accessed by turning off this on the east side of the river. Postcode for SatNav is SA65 9NB.

Parking

There is limited parking along the quay and further parking is possible along the main road where it comes down the hill from Upper Fishguard to the bridge.

Water access

Access from seaward is easy after rounding the main breakwater. Beacons mark some offlying rocks on the west side of the entrance. Mooring alongside is difficult because of the many frapes attached to the permanent moorings. Contact the harbourmaster or the yacht club for a mooring.

Fishguard Bay Yacht Club plaque

Facilities
Nothing in Lower Fishguard except the yacht club on the quay, but full town facilities in Upper Fishguard.

More information
Yacht Club www.fbyc.org.uk
Harbourmaster ☎ 01348 873369 or 07775 523846

Comments
Fishguard harbour is tucked away in what seems an almost forgotten corner of the area, with the main road traffic rushing past with hardly a glance at the history close by.

The quay with the buildings used in the Under Milk Wood film still retains its traditional feel

Newport

This is the 'other' Newport, the one in Pembrokeshire, not the shipping port in South Wales. It has a long history dating back to the 11th century, but despite its name the port could date back even further. The Blue Stones of Stonehenge originated from the Prescelly Mountains just above Newport and it is possible they were shipped out from the river to the sea journey to the south.

The port at Newport was in use for shipping wool back in the 11th century when Newport was a major centre for the wool trade. It lies on the estuary of the River Nevern with its entrance sheltered to a certain extent by Dinas Head to the west, but, like most of the river harbours in West Wales, it has suffered from having a shifting sand bar across the entrance. The wool trade declined in the 16th centuray when the plague struck the area but it built up again a century later when the current harbour (called The Parrog) was built. This harbour with its stone walls and piers, faces west with direct entry from the river; outside along the river bank the quay walls extend eastwards to provide additional quay space. The cargoes handled at the harbour were the usual mix of coal, limestone and timber coming in and mainly farm produce going out.

Stone was also exported from quarries on the Prescelly Mountains. The construction of the quay walls uses flat stones laid vertically (in contrast to the normal horizontal position) and this gives the walls a unique appearance. These stones are slate, which was also one of the exports from the harbour. Even the steps let into the quay walls use the same vertical stone layout.

In addition to the quay walls, history can also be seen in the row of lime kilns adjacent to the car park and there is an old warehouse on the quay (one of five that were there originally) which has now been converted into the headquarters of the Newport Boat Club, reflecting the mainly leisure use of the harbour these days. Further to seaward of the harbour there were shipyards in the past and Newport is also reported to have been the home of many ships' captains.

Vertical laid stones form the steps in the quay

There is still a strong feeling of history about the harbour and its surroundings and, despite the challenging bar across the entrance to the river, the harbour supports a significant number of leisure and angling boats during the summer.

Access by road

The harbour itself is not signposted as such but from the main A487 coast road that passes through the town turn down Parrog Road, which is located to the west of the town. The quay is about half a mile down this road on the right. Postcode for SatNav is SA42 0RP.

Parking

There is parking on the quay area by the lime kilns and further parking associated with the boat club.

Water access

The entrance channel is marked by buoys but you need to be close in to pick them out. Best to enter near high water on a rising tide. Contact the boat club for a mooring but tenders can tie up or be hauled out by the boat club.

Facilities

Newport has all the facilities of a small town with pubs, hotels, cafés and shops but it is half a mile from the harbour.

More information

www.newportpembs.co.uk
www.newportboatclub.co.uk

Comments

The harbour area itself is removed from the main part of the town of Newport, probably because there was a risk of flooding of the low-lying land near the river. The lack of any signposting to the harbour seems to suggest that the town has lost interest in the harbour which was responsible for its prosperity in the past, but it nevertheless is well worth a visit.

The small dock basin and entrance channel with the Boat Club on the left

Cardigan

Restoration work has involved this new quay wall and floating pontoon

Located near the mouth of the River Teifi, Cardigan was a major port in the past, with the town itself developing around its location as the first crossing point over the river. As a port Cardigan ranked as the main Welsh port in the 18th century, with more ships registered here than at Cardiff and Swansea. However, it fell into decline as the river silted up and the railway came to take away much of the trade at the latter end of the 19th century.

The port developed on the river some three miles in from the sea and there were wharves that can still be seen along both sides of the river just downstream from the bridge. The castle located at the northern end of the bridge dominates the bridge and harbour area and the town was originally a defensive walled settlement around the castle. The entrance to the river between Cemaes Head and Cardigan Island faces almost north so it was protected from the prevailing westerlies, but the shallow bar across the entrance could create dangerous seas in adverse conditions and provided a constant challenge to ships entering the harbour. It was mainly the silting and constant changes of this bar that were responsible for the decline of the port.

At its peak in the 18th century there were 314 ships registered at the port and it was also a base for a large fishing fleet exploiting the Irish Sea herring. These herring constituted one of the exports, with salt being brought in to preserve the herring; other exports were slate and farm produce. Other imports were coal and building materials in addition to the salt. This was a thriving harbour, with five shipyards both in the town and further downstream at Llandudoch.

Today the harbour area around the town only hosts a few vessels, mainly yachts, but the main marine business of the area has moved downstream to a point just inside the entrance on the east side where there are extensive yacht moorings and services. At Cardigan itself some of the original warehouses on the west side of the river have been restored and further downstream on the east side the

main car park is located on what was one of the main port areas, with the stone quays still in place.

Access by road

There is now a bypass around the town for the A487; by turning into the town you arrive at the bridge across the river and the castle where much of the old port is located. Postcode for SatNav is SA43 1HR.

Parking

The main car park is on the east side downstream from the bridge and is signposted after crossing the bridge. It is a pay and display car park.

Water access

The entrance across the bar is constantly changing and it is a good idea to get local advice before attempting the entrance. The main mooring area is near Gwbert on Sea but there are also moorings up the river. It is possible to explore upstream of the bridge by tender on a rising tide and there is a pontoon established close by the bridge.

Facilities

The full facilities of a county town are available with more pubs and shops at some of the small villages along the estuary.

More information

www.tourism.ceredigion.gov.uk
Teifi Boating Club www.teifiboatingclub.co.uk
Mooring master ℡ 01239 613966

Comments

The town had rather turned its back on the river, with a sense of decay amongst some of the riverside buildings, but now there are plans to revive the waterfront area and this can already be seen on the east side near the bridge where the quay has been restored and a floating pontoon installed, with plans for a riverside walk.

Restored warehouses on the south side near the bridge

The entrance to the river with the breaking shallow bar in the distance

Llangrannog

Llangrannog is a stunningly beautiful cove that the world almost seems to have passed by. It became a harbour partly because of its north-facing aspect that offered shelter from the prevailing winds and partly because of the way in which the headlands that enclose it on each side provide additional shelter. This is a purely natural harbour where the ships coming in would be beached at low water and discharge their cargoes into horses and carts for transport into the village or to the farms up country. The harbour was also home to a fishing fleet which was mainly exploiting the Irish Sea herring.

The village and its curved beach are located where the River Hawen makes its steep way down to the sea, with the village situated in the almost ravine-like valley. To the west there is another, smaller, river in a similar steep valley that also finds the sea in the small bay. So steep is the valley that there is a small waterfall in the village and historically the village

The restored limekiln on the quay

*View from the slipway
looking to sea*

was above this waterfall, with the lower village being a later development when the maritime trade developed. Old photos show that the main area where the sailing ships came into the beach was on the west side, where they could tuck in under the shelter of the steep headland. One old photo shows three ships dried out on the beach at the same time, which demonstrates the importance of this small harbour. Limestone and coal were the main cargoes brought in by these ships and there is an old lime kiln at the top of the slipway, so the cargoes did not have far to travel. This slipway is the main access to the beach and it would have provided the access to the ships for the horses and carts.

In keeping with so many of these small Welsh river harbours there was a shipbuilding industry, but it is reported that at Llangrannog the ships were actually built on the beach above the high-water mark, which demonstrates a lot of faith in the weather.

Today Llangrannog focuses almost entirely on the tourist trade but there is an active boating association which is responsible for the small-boat storage area at the top of the slipway and the launching facilities on the slipway itself.

Access by road

Coming from the north turn off the main A487 coast road on to the B4321 to Llangrannog. From the south it is the B4334 that leads to the village down a series of hairpin bends. Postcode for SatNav is SA44 6SP.

Parking

There is free parking at the top of the village (with a considerable walk to the beach) but there is a pay and display car park virtually in the middle of the beach area.

Water access

There is a patch of rocks just off the west headland of the bay which need a wide berth, otherwise it is straight into the sandy beach where landing by small boat is possible. When anchoring off in water deep

The beautiful secluded bay where ships would have been beached to unload

enough to stay afloat you lose the shelter of the headlands.

Facilities

Two pubs, the Pentre Arms and the Ship Inn, are located close to the beach and there are cafés and a shop.

More information

www.llangrannog.org.uk
Llangrannog Boating and Angling Association
Email dijones@ginetiq.com

Comments

In the summer this is an active boating area and in settled conditions boats can moor off the sheltered beach. The village is well worth a visit as a location that the world seems almost to have passed by. In strong winds you can get a feel of what conditions might have been like when trying to beach ships here.

Aberaeron

Located at the mouth of the River Aeron, Aberaeron developed for many years as a typical Welsh river mouth port. By facing northwest there was a certain level of protection from the prevailing winds and it was very active in the Irish Sea herring fishery. In the 17th century Aberaeron coastal trade developed, with coal, lime and salt coming in and mainly farm produce, salted herring and some lead ore from the mines near Lampeter going out.

Like many of the river harbours there was a recurring problem with flooding and a Harbour Act of 1807 allowed for the construction of two stone piers jutting out into the sea to control the channel of the harbour mouth. Following this development a local landowner decided that the time was ripe to develop the village into a sizeable town with a harbour to match to make it the focal point of trade along this coast. The first section of the harbour to be developed was what is now the inner harbour on the north side of the river, which offered excellent shelter. This section was completed in 1811 and then the excavation and development of what is now the main part of the harbour was completed five years later. This harbour development was part of a master plan to create a new town around the harbour and this can be seen to good advantage today, making Aberaeron a major tourist attraction. Back when the harbour was being built it was used to import much of the stone used for the

construction work and there were lime kilns on either side of the harbour to supply the lime needed by both the local farmers and for use as mortar for the local construction work.

Shipbuilding had been a part of the port virtually since its inception, but with the development of the new harbour and with the washing away in a flood of the shipyard at nearby Aberarth, shipbuilding became a major activity, with over 70 vessels reportedly built in the Aberaeron yards using wood sourced from the local forests.

In 1860 the Aeron Express was built, a wire-supported hand-operated cable car that was used to transport workers across the harbour in a little two-man carriage. In 1911 the railway was extended south from Aberystwyth to Aberaeron and Cardigan and it was this that started the decline in the trade of the harbour.

Access by road

Aberaeron lies on the main A487 coast road, which forms the main street of the town with the harbour on the west side. Postcode for SatNav is SA46 0DP.

Parking

There is pay and display parking around the harbour on both sides, with a main car park out near the south pier which is used for boat storage in the winter.

Plaque in memory of the building of the S W Pier

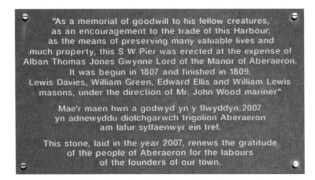

"As a memorial of goodwill to his fellow creatures, as an encouragement to the trade of this Harbour, as the means of preserving many valuable lives and much property, this S W Pier was erected at the expense of Alban Thomas Jones Gwynne Lord of the Manor of Aberaeron. It was begun in 1807 and finished in 1809. Lewis Davies, William Green, Edward Ellis and William Lewis masons, under the direction of Mr. John Wood mariner"

Mae'r maen hwn a godwyd yn y flwyddyn 2007 yn adnewyddu diolchgarwch trigolion Aberaeron am lafur sylfaenwyr ein tref.

This stone, laid in the year 2007, renews the gratitude of the people of Aberaeron for the labours of the founders of our town.

The entrance channel into the harbour at low water

Water access

Straight in from seaward between the piers, although there is a submerged breakwater extending out from the south pier which is marked by a green beacon. There is temporary berthing alongside the quay wall on the north side, with convenient access to pubs and hotels and longer-term moorings are available on application to the harbourmaster and the yacht club. A floating pontoon is located on the south side just inside the pier.

Facilities

There are the full facilities of a small town, including pubs, shops, hotels and restaurants/cafés.

More information

www.aberaeron-westwales.co.uk
Aberaeron Yacht Club www.aberaeronyachtclub.org
Harbourmaster ☎ 01545 571645 or 0797 4669036

Comments

Today the harbour dries out at low water and it is mainly used by leisure craft, with a few fishing boats operating from the harbour. The swell that comes into the harbour in stronger winds when the tide is high means that boats in the harbour lie at moorings rather than alongside the quays, although there is the beginning of a marina in the more sheltered inner harbour. Today Aberaeron is a much more developed harbour and a total contrast to the many other harbours along this exposed coastline. It still retains a magical air.

Ynyslas

Ynyslas is little more than a tidal creek leading off the main Dovey Estuary and as a harbour it only served the local area, with the main ports of Aberdovey and Aberystwyth being the focus of trade in the area. However, whilst most of the ports in this area suffered once the railways came, Ynyslas benefitted because the railway ran close by the harbour when it was built in 1867 and there were sidings from the main line right alongside the wharves on the riverside. This meant that Ynyslas became an important transshipment port for a short time, the main export being farm produce from the fertile plains on the hinterland (one of the few areas of flat farm land in this part of Wales). It was also used to import coal and fertilisers for the local communities.

Before the railway arrived on the northern side of the Dovey Estuary there was a ferry operating from Ynyslas to Aberdovey to save the long journey around by land, and a branch line of the railway was built to serve this ferry. Ynyslas is the only harbour on the south side of the Dovey Estuary and so it served quite a large area of hinterland; although it is very tidal, with a twisting entrance channel through the sandbanks along the Afon Leri channel, it worked well for the trading schooners. The remains of the old wooden wharves can still be seen downstream of the modern quay but they are in a state of decay and may well disappear if there is any expansion of the current boatyard.

Unlike in many of the harbours along the Welsh coast there was never any shipbuilding established at Ynyslas, mainly because there was no ready source of timber in the hinterland. However, this has changed in modern times and the main feature of the current harbour is the boatyard that was established in the 1960s. The dominant construction hall and the concrete retaining walls saw the building of a number of fishing and passenger boats, including some that now operate on the River Thames. Boatbuilding has now stopped at Ynyslas but the yard is still very active, mainly with yacht repair

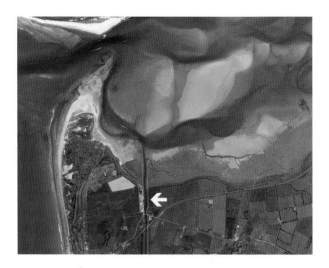

work and boat storage, so the harbour is now being transformed into a minor yachting centre.

The whole area of the peninsula on which Ynyslas stands has now been transformed into a wildlife and leisure centre which includes a golf course and caravan sites on the sand dunes, while fishing and yachting are becoming increasingly popular. Ynyslas was once an island that was cut off at high tide. The creek on which the town stands runs more or less north–south parallel to the seashore outside and the river drains much of the low-lying land that forms the fertile plains of the farmland.

Access by road

The B4353 coast road from Borth in the south to Machynlleth in the north runs close by the current boatyard. Postcode for SatNav is SY24 5JU.

Parking

No designated parking except in the boatyard itself.

Water access

The Dovey Estuary is well marked by buoys and the channel to Ynyslas is marked by buoys in the summer.

Facilities

None apart from those of the boatyard.

More information

www.visitmidwales.co.uk
www.ynyslasboatyard.co.uk

Comments

The harbour at Ynyslas does nothing to attract visitors but there is a sense of history about the place, although the modern boatyard facilities seem almost alien to such a peaceful location.

The harbour channel at low water with some of the old timber quays on the centre. Aberdovey is in the distance

Penmaenpool

Penmaenpool, located in fantastic scenery on the Mawddach Estuary that flows out to sea at Barmouth, has proved to be adaptable through the ages. This small hamlet supported fishing in the estuary and adjacent farming but it started to expand in the 15th century as a shipbuilding centre. The attraction for locating it at this inland location was, firstly, that it did not impinge on the crowded fishing and cargo quays at Barmouth, and, secondly, the ready access to shipbuilding timber from the nearby forests.

The current George III hotel, which is the main building in Penmaenpool, was developed from two buildings, one of which was a ship chandlers and the other a pub, two vital ingredients of any shipyard. The buildings date back to 1650 and they were connected to form the hotel in 1890. The shipyard probably existed up till around the 1850s, when ships started to be built with iron rather than wood and steam was taking over from sail. The railway came through here in the late 1800s and closed down in 1964, with part of the station buildings being added to the hotel.

Penmaenpool is located where the estuary channel sweeps round close to the shore so that there is deep water along the frontage here, which would have made it perfect for the shipyards. Oak was the main shipbuilding material and it is said that there are no oak trees left in the wooded slopes behind the hotel because the shipyards took them all.

A notable feature of Penmaenpool is the wooden toll bridge across the river which was opened around 1879 to replace a ferry. This was the scene of a major boating accident in 1966 when a tripper boat, *The Prince of Wales*, coming up from Barmouth, hit the bridge when turning in the river and 15 of the 39 passengers were drowned.

Gold was mined in the hills on the north side of the estuary here and the remains of the mines and the processing equipment can still be seen.

The George III that was once a ship's chandlers on the quay

Road access

Turn off the A 493 south estuary road where Penmaenpool is signposted. Postcode for SatNav is LL40 1YD.

Parking

A car park has been established just to the east of the bridge to serve the walking trail here.

Water access

Access is up the estuary channels from Barmouth on a rising tide. The Ordnance Survey map gives a better idea of where the access channels lie, but this can be updated by contacting the Barmouth harbour master. It is possible to moor alongside at a landing with steps close by the hotel at high water. There are a few moorings in the river.

Facilities

The welcoming hotel is the only facility here and it provides food and drink in historical surroundings.

More information

Merioneth Yacht Club ✆ 01341 280000
www.merionethyachtclub.co.uk
Barmouth harbourmaster ✆ 01341 280671
The George III hotel www.georgethethird.co.uk

The wooden toll bridge that was the scene of a boat disaster in 1966

Pensarn Harbour

This tiny harbour makes you realise just how important sea transport was before the railways and road were developed in Wales. The quay is located on what is one of the most difficult harbours to navigate in Wales and yet it was developed because the sea access was vital.

Pensarn stands on what was the estuary of the River Artro, which has a west-facing entrance that is wide open to the storms of the Irish Sea. The estuary has changed considerably over the years with various land reclamation projects. In the 19th century a landowner diverted the channel of the river for reclamation work and this created the new entrance further north, where it is today. The river winds across the low-lying land, with the estuary gradually narrowing as it approaches Llanbedr; the quay at Pensarn is situated at the point where the estuary becomes a river.

This quay with its warehouse was used to bring in the usual cargoes of coal and other imports such as limestone and to ship out farm produce. There was another quay closer to the estuary entrance, where the yacht club buildings now stand, but Pensarn was much closer to the destinations and source of the cargoes passing through the harbour. It is thought that the harbour at Pensarn dates back to medieval times, but its death knell sounded when the railway

came to the region and there is a station located immediately behind the quay. The main coast road also runs close by.

Today the stone quay at Pensarn is still in use as an outdoor pursuits centre run by the Christian Mountain Centre, and there are yacht moorings alongside the east side of the quay. A lime kiln which served the quay has now been built into the residential block that is part of this centre. In addition to this, the harbour is active for yachting, but a major storm in 2010 demonstrated the vulnerability of the harbour, many yachts being wrecked inside the harbour.

Access by road

Turn off the main A496 coast road at the signs for the railway station. Access to the activities centre is across a self-operated level crossing. Postcode for SatNav is LL45 2HS.

Parking

There is a yacht club car park by the level crossing but otherwise very limited road parking.

Yachts moored on the quay where once trading ships discharged

The stone quay at Pensarn juts out into the estuary

Water access

The entrance channel runs north parallel to the coast from the actual entrance through the sand dunes and the sandbanks move around, particularly after storms. Contact the harbourmaster or the yacht club for advice and moorings. There is a pontoon alongside the quay operated by the outdoor centre.

Facilities

No public facilities on the quay; village facilities in Pensarn.

More information

Llanbedr and Pensarn Yacht Club www.lpyc.org.uk
Harbourmaster ☎ 01341 241628
Email Peter_stephens@talk21.com

Comments

It is good to see this ancient quay still in use even though that use is far removed from what it was originally designed for. This is a quite wild and remote part of Wales but there is considerable farmland in the catchment area.

Borth-y-Gest

The harbour at Borth-y-Gest is overshadowed by the main port at Porthmadog just upriver, but at one time Borth-y-Gest was the more important place because it was one end of a crossing route across the treacherous sands of the Dwyryd Estuary towards what is now Portmeirion. At that time Borth-y-Gest was a sheltered bay that was probably the main harbour on the estuary, used for bringing in cargoes of coal, limestone and produce but things changed when The Cob, the long embankment across the upper estuary, was built in the 19th century. That changed the tides and currents in the estuary dramatically and was used to form the deep water port at Porthmadog so the harbour business moved upriver.

The bay where ships would moor to discharge their cargoes before Porthmadog was developed

The importance of Borth-y-Gest as a port can be judged by the legend which suggests that Prince Madog set sail from here in the 12th century to discover America. There is no hard evidence of this Welshman discovering America before Columbus, but the harbour must have been significant in those days.

Borth-y-Gest did not lose out entirely when trade (particularly the slate trade) was established at Porthmadog, because Borth-y-Gest then became an important shipbuilding centre and there is evidence that there were four shipyards around the harbour.

Today at the southern extremity of the bay close by the main channel there is a wide space cut through the rocks, with the remains of what might have been a quay or slipway and perhaps the only reminder left of the past shipping activity. Now the harbour is surrounded by a sea wall that serves to support the road and the car park and the harbour is used by yachts and small craft mainly in the summer months. The stream that flows into the harbour at its northern corner and which probably carved out the bay forms a sort of deeper-water channel and there is some evidence of the remains of stone walls in this area which could have been wharves in the past.

Access by road

After leaving Porthmadog head south; follow the signs to Borth-y-Gest and drop down the hill into the village and the road around the harbour. Postcode for SatNav is LL49 9TR.

Parking

Free parking along the road around the harbour and in a car park on the south side of the harbour front.

Water access

First you have to negotiate the challenging entrance to the estuary across the bar near Harlech Point close to high water and then follow the channel that mainly hugs the northwest side of the estuary. The harbour at Borth-y-Gest dries out completely at low water. There are many moorings in the harbour and on a yacht it is probably best to continue upriver to the facilities at Porthmadog where most of the moorings also dry out. Take advice from harbourmaster before entering

Facilities

Borth-y-Gest has little to offer in terms of facilities but just around the corner upriver is the Madog Boatyard, and of course Porthmadog has all the facilities of a town.

More information

Madoc Yacht Club www.madocyachtclub.com
Porthmadog harbourmaster ☎ 01766 512927
Madog Boatyard www.boats-wales.com
Tourist office Porthmadog ☎ 01766 512981

Comments

Today Borth-y-Gest is a tranquil place, with fantastic views across the water to the mountains of Snowdonia. The harbour and village are slightly off the beaten track, hence the lack of facilities, and the village seems happy to remain so.

The remains of what was probably one of the old slipways

Cricceth

The history of both Cricceth and the modern town are dominated by the castle, with the harbour taking very much second place. The castle, located on its towering rocky headland, looks down on both the town and the harbour and it is easy to see why this site was chosen. It can also act as a control point for the river entrance to nearby Porthmadog so the castle would dominate both the land and the sea. However, the small harbour at Cricceth was important for bringing in coal and other requirements to the town and ships would have landed on the sheltered beach underneath the castle. There is no record of when the breakwater was added to the harbour defences but it is likely that it was first constructed from the stones and boulders that were cleared from the beach to create a safe

The harbour lies under the shelter of the dominant castle

beaching place for the ships. The harbour at Criccieth served quite a large hinterland because it offered a safe alternative to the dangerous river entrance nearby and there was little in the way of a port at Porthmadog until the 19th century, when the long embankment across the estuary was built to reclaim land from the sea. That in turn focussed the current and created a deeper-water channel to make Porthmadog the favoured port.

Criccieth reverted largely to serve as a harbour for its fishing boats and the occasional cargo ship but once road and rail links improved, particularly with the coming of the railway, Criccieth became a fishing harbour and more recently the sheltered bay became a base for yachts and boating in the summer months.

The lifeboat house is now the focus of the harbour, but the all-weather lifeboat was taken away in 1931 and now the station houses an inshore lifeboat to provide coverage for the Dwyfor Estuary. Criccieth may be a small harbour but there is a long tradition of Criccieth men becoming sailors for both coastal and foreign-going ships and the town has long been the retirement home for many ships' captains .

The stony beach with the lifeboat house painted red

Access by road

The A497 coast road passes through Criccieth, with the harbour tucked inside the east side of the castle after you pass under the railway bridge. Postcode for SatNav is LL52 0DN.

Parking

Limited free parking along the seafront and in the town.

Water access

Straight in with no offlying dangers, with the castle providing a mark. Anchorage under the shelter of the castle (but possibly crowded in the summer) and landing on the beach inside the breakwater, which dries at low water.

Facilities

All the facilities of a small town, including pubs, hotels, cafés and shops.

More information

www.criccieth.co.uk

Comments

Criccieth gets very busy in the summer as a holiday resort but in the winter it is as quiet as if the world has passed it by. Despite its strong sea-going connections the harbour itself does not appear to be a major focus of town life.

Plaque on the lifeboat house

Abersoch

Located on the east side of the Lleyn Peninsula, St Tudwal's Roads offers excellent shelter for shipping except for winds from the east, and the harbour at Abersoch is even more sheltered. This is a tiny river harbour that in the past was home port to small fishing boats; it is thought that the harbour may have been the landing point for pilgrims who were visiting many of the holy sites in the area. There were also lead workings at nearby Llanengan so Abersoch would have been the nearest port for exporting the mineral. Other exports were farm produce and imports were mainly coal for local use.

The outer harbour beyond the narrow river entrance provided good protection in most conditions and further protection was offered when the outer breakwater was built in the early 20th century.

Today you do not see a lot of history at Abersoch except in the row of cottages that border the south side of the inner harbour and there have been considerable developments to turn Abersoch harbour into a major water sports centre. Much of the inner harbour has been in-filled to create hard standings for the two main boatyards and this in turn has created quay walls inside the harbour. Despite this development there is still a traditional feel to the harbour, where the road bridge over the River Soch forms the inner limit of the harbour and the main channel is forced through a narrow entrance then continues close to the outer breakwater. What used to be a low sandy spit marking the north side of the river entrance has now been transformed into the lifeboat house and launching slipway for the inshore lifeboat.

Access by road

Direct access along the A499 coast road from Pwllheli. Postcode for SatNav is LL53 7AP.

The entrance to the harbour at low water

Parking

Very difficult in the summer. There is very limited street parking and several hotels have parking.

Water access

The main entrance channel flows close to the line of the outer breakwater and there are mooring buoys along the line of the channel, but entrance is only feasible towards high water. However, there are mooring buoys in much of the area off Abersoch. There is a yacht club jetty to the south of the breakwater as a landing point from the moorings. Anchoring is difficult because of the extensive moorings that are laid in the bay.

Facilities

There are pubs, hotels, cafés and restaurants plus a variety of shops in the town.

Abersoch Land and Sea and Abersoch Boatyard provide facilities for boats and the South Caernarvonshire Yacht Club welcomes visiting yachtsmen.

More information

South Caernarvonshire Yacht Club
www.scyc.co.uk
Email info@scyc.co.uk
① 01758 712 338
Tourist office ① 01758 712929

Comments

The main village is on the south side of the harbour, where the narrow streets have houses and hotels and all the trappings of a busy holiday resort. The modern boatyards that handle yachts and small boats have taken over from the old shipyards that in the past would build trading ships for working along the coast. Despite the modern developments this is still a fascinating small port but it is best visited in the winter when it is quieter.

Abersoch looks peaceful in the winter but is a hive of activity in the summer months

The channel into the harbour with the lifeboat house under the trees

Porth Nefyn and Porthdinllaen

These two harbours in adjacent bays on the north side of the Lleyn Peninsula are real gems of hidden harbours. There is vehicle access to both harbours but for Porthdinllaen it is along a private road only accessible to local residents and members of the golf club, whilst at Porth Nefyn you have to drive across the beach to get to the harbour. So these are harbours that you have to walk to, but although they are now well off the beaten track, history indicates just how close they came to being a major British port.

When trade to Ireland developed and the railways started to create access to more remote areas, Porthdinllaen was promoted as being the place to locate the ferry terminal for the Irish packet ships. It was only because the required Act of Parliament did not get sufficient support that the ferry terminal was actually built at Holyhead instead. So these two small harbours remain in almost original form, although the harbour wall at Porth Nefyn has been reconstructed.

Both of these harbours were originally used as bases for the fishing fleets that exploited the prolific Irish Sea herring fisheries and it was the landings from these fisheries that led to the importing of the large quantities of salt used to preserve the fish. Coal

The rebuilt harbour wall at Porth Nefyn with access only along the beach

was also imported for local use. Porthdinllaen, with its north-extending peninsula, was a significant port of refuge in sailing ship days, offering virtually the only place to shelter from storms along this exposed coastline. Inshore there is a short stone breakwater to offer protection to any vessel landing on the beach, whilst at Porth Nefyn there is a much more substantial breakwater because the headland close by this port does not offer the same level of protection. Both ports were noted for their shipbuilding in the past but it is hard to visualise the level of past activity in the idyllic present-day surroundings on this quite beautiful stretch of coastline. Today just a few fishing boats operate from both harbours.

Access by road

There is no public vehicle access to Porthdinllaen along the access road running north from Morfa Nefyn so there is a walk of a mile to access the village. Postcode for SatNav is LL53 6DA.

Porth Nefyn is equally remote, with access to the beach down a road from a point just west of the village of Nefyn. This road turns through three hairpins and the final access to the harbour is along the top of the beach and is not recommended.

Porthdinllaen stretches alone the beach below the cliffs

Parking

There is a National Trust pay car park close by the crossroads where the road out to Porthdinllaen starts. At Porth Nefyn there is a car park with around 20 spaces just above the beach on the road down.

Water access

At Porthdinllaen round the beacon on Careg y Chwislen that marks the outer rocks before turning into the harbour area. Once inside it is possible to anchor off the village but beware of rocks to the south. Anchorage off is also possible at Porth Nefyn but the shelter is not so good here. At high tide there may be temporary mooring alongside the harbour wall when conditions are settled.

Facilities

There is a pub, the Ty Coch Inn, at Porthdinllaen but otherwise there are village facilities in Nefyn and Morfa Nefyn.

More information

www.walesinfo.com
Porthdinllaen harbourmaster ☎ 01758 721 643

Comments

These harbours represent the north Wales coastline at its beautiful best and they are both well worth the walk it takes to get to them. The breakwater at Porth Nefyn has been restored in recent years to offer better protection for the fishing boats.

*The wide sweep of the beach
with the Golf Club above*

Trefor

The harbour at Trefor is dominated by the stone and wooden jetty that juts out from the shore but at the shore end of the main jetty there is a small, partly enclosed harbour that was probably there long before the main jetty was built. This earlier harbour tucked in under the shelter of the nearby headland would have served the local fishing boats, but it was the demand for the high quality granite from the quarry on the slopes of the nearby Yr Eifl mountain that led to the development of the harbour as we see it today.

However, the present-day harbour was not the first here to be developed to handle the granite exports and if you walk along the coast a short distance out towards the headland you will find the remains of a stone quay that would been accessible to ships at high water where they would dry out to

load the stone. The demand for the granite and the need for a more reliable means of transport for it led to the development of, first, the stone jetty reaching out into deeper waters and offering a measure of shelter to ships that would come alongside, and then later the wooden extension that angles out into even deeper water, where larger ships could be accommodated. They would have come in and been loaded probably over just one high-water period.

The quarry opened in 1850 and a railway was built in 1865 to create a more efficient means of bringing the stone down to the harbour. This railway was closed down in the 20th century in favour of road transport and the quarry and the use of the harbour were finally closed in 1960. The old harbour would have seen sailing ships making landfall here, but the more modern jetty was built to allow the larger steam and then motor ships to come in to load the stone, indicative of the high demand for this particular granite. The granite was used mainly for making road sets and even for the curling stones used for sport, but later the stone was crushed for road building.

Today the small harbour is used by sea angling boats and the pier itself is in great demand by anglers, with the good beaches making this area a great family place.

The old section of this harbour with it stone walls and bollards

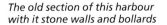

Access by road

There are two turnings off the A499 coast road to Trefor and then in the village a signposted road leads to the harbour road. Postcode for SatNav is LL54 5LU.

Parking

Limited free parking on the quay and a small car part off the access road

Water access

Straight in after rounding the Yr Eifl headland; it is possible to lie alongside the stone section of the jetty but this dries out at low water. Otherwise anchor off and come in by tender.

Facilities

Nothing at the harbour but village facilities up the road

More information

www.walesinfo.com
Porthdinllaen harbourmaster ☏ 01758 721643

Comments

There is so much history here, but Trefor now has an abandoned feel about it. Nevertheless it is still a great place to visit for a picnic or just for the views, with none of the trappings of modern life such as seaside facilities in sight.

The modern section of the jetty runs out into deeper water

Caernarfon

The top of the harbour offices on the quay speaks of past prosperity

Caernarfon only just qualifies as a hidden harbour, and only because the harbour area is hidden behind the dominant castle. This famous castle dates back to the 13th century and the first port was located on quays built alongside it. It is probable that much of the stone used for building the castle was brought by ship into the River Seiont that now forms the old port of Caernarfon. In the early days of the port ships discharged alongside onto the stone wharves, or if they were too big for the port they anchored off and cargoes were transshipped into lighters.

Caernarfon hit the big time as a port towards the end of the 17th century when the slate quarries at Nantile and Dinorwic were opened up and the Port Trust was formed in 1793 to develop the port for exporting slate. The Trust's first development was the building of the new wharf alongside the castle. This was opened in 1817 and the port obviously prospered because the Trust built an imposing office alongside the wharf in 1840. In the 1860s the Trust constructed the Victoria Dock along the waterfront of the Menai Strait to make better facilities available, but by then the writing was on the wall because the railway was extended to the town in 1852.

In addition to being a major port for cargo with coal and produce coming in, the port was also a major exporter of slate. Later, timber was brought into the port from North America and the slate was taken out in a valuable two-way trade, but the port was in decline with the railway running right alongside the dock area. Caernarfon kept going into the steam era, with passenger steamers running here from Liverpool, but today the port mainly caters for yachts and a few fishing boats.

The Caernarfon Harbour Trust is responsible for the whole of the Menai Strait from the Britannia Bridge in the east to the Caernarfon Bar in the west. In addition to cargoes Caernarfon, like many of the harbours in this region, was a major shipbuilding port.

Access by road

The town is well signposted and you come to the Slate Quay when approaching from the west. From the east the castle is a good landmark. Postcode for SatNav is LL55 2PB.

Parking

A pay and display car park is located on Slate Quay.

Water access

Across Caernarfon Bar and into the Menai Straits then head towards the Victoria Dock entrance before picking up the fairway buoy that leads into the buoyed channel to the river entrance. Sound your horn for the bridge to open.

Facilities

All the facilities of a major town. The Royal Welsh Yacht Club in the town welcomes visiting yachtsmen.

More information

www.visitcaernarfon.com
Caernarfon Harbour Trust
www.caernarfon-hbr.demon.co.uk
☎ 01286 672118
Email enquiries@caernarfonharbour.co.uk

Comments

There are facilities for yachts in both the river alongside the Slate Quay and in Victoria Dock and Caernarfon is one of the most dramatic harbours in the region for visitors by both land and sea. A pedestrian swing bridge now crosses the entrance to the river and forms part of a coastal walk.

The magnificent castle dominates the quay below

Tal y Foel and the Mermaid Inn

Tal y Foel and the Mermaid Inn share a common heritage in that they are both places where a ferry used to run across the Menai Strait to Caernarfon on the mainland.

Tal y Foel is now a silted-up harbour with the remains of the small landing area still visible and it is only accessible by land down a private road. It was probably the silting up of this harbour that was the reason behind the move up the Menai Strait to the Mermaid Inn location. The ferry service ran from Tal y Foel from 1464 right through to 1852 when the terminal was moved to the Mermaid Inn. It operated until 1952 when the road infrastructure had improved to the point where the ferry was redundant.

In its heyday the ferry would carry people and produce from the fertile lands of Anglesey to the markets at Caernarfon and also workers to the quarries on the mainland. The ferry operated across the difficult waters of the Menai Strait and in strong winds it must have been a treacherous voyage.

Today the small enclosed dock at Mermaid Inn that created a safe landing for the ferry still exists in private hands, acting as a dock for a sea angling boat and a few small craft. The Mermaid Inn has also closed, so the thought of a tempting drink on the waterfront overlooking the Strait is not feasible. What used to be the inn is now also in private hands and although it looks as if it is being converted into

a smart B&B the Mermaid Inn Hotel signs can still be seen on its wall. There is a nearby equestrian centre that offers farm accommodation and historic tours of the area on horseback, but for anything in the way of sustenance you need to head back to the villages on the main road.

The remains of a pier extending out into deeper water can be seen about a quarter of a mile to the north of the Mermaid Inn dock. The area is worth a visit, if only for the tremendous views across the Strait to Caernarfon and the mountains of Snowdonia.

Access by road

From the main A4080 turn towards the waterfront on to the B4419, which is signposted to Foel but not numbered. Postcode for SatNav is LL61 6LQ.

Parking

Free parking along the waterfront in unmarked areas.

Water access

At high water you can head across the shoals on this side of the Strait but towards low water you need to follow the inshore channel, which is marked by mooring buoys, towards the cluster of houses on the shore.

Half tide rocks offer some protection to this tiny harbour

The remains of the old wooden jetty at Tal y Foel

Facilities

None on the waterfront but shops and pubs in the villages on the main road.

More information

Tal y Foel Riding School www.tal-y-foel.co.uk

Comments

This is an idyllic place with its stunning views across the Straits so it is a great shame that the Mermaid Inn could not remain viable. With no food or drink available this is nevertheless still a great place for a picnic because of the views and its isolation.

What used to be the ferry harbour is now home to a private deep sea angling boat

Aberffraw

Aberffraw has never been an important port, mainly because of its challenging entrance. It is wide open to the prevailing southwesterly winds and the evidence of this comes in the form of the extensive sand dunes that extend over the whole of the eastern side of the entrance.

The River Ffraw that forms the harbour hugs the western shore and the sand dunes and the river now live in reasonable and stable harmony except for the shoals in the entrance, which can change after adverse weather. So the port was mainly used by small craft to bring in various commodities and the exports would have been mainly farm produce and perhaps coal which would have come from the coal mines at Malltraeth down the road, although there is no evidence of this except is the apparent stone wharves on the river that are now supporting homes.

The port was significant in the Middle Ages but silting of the entrance after the Great Storm of 1331 and the encroaching sand dunes reduced its importance. The village of Aberffraw has a huge history as one of the most important places in Wales when it was the capital of the Principality of North Wales in AD870. There was a castle in the village but no trace now remains and Aberffraw has returned to being a sleepy hamlet.

The beautiful old Packhorse Bridge spans the river

Part of the history of the village is reflected in the ancient stone packhorse bridge that spans the river in the village: this is a wonderful example of this type of bridge now it has been fully restored, framing the upper reaches of the river

Access by road

On the A4080 coast road that runs along the south shores of Anglesey. Postcode for SatNav is LL63 5YU.

Parking

In the village and along the river edge. Also parking on the east side of the bridge for access to the sand dunes and the beach.

Water access

There is a possible anchorage at the entrance to the river that can be identified by the historic white painted chapel on an island to the west of the entrance. The river itself and the village are best explored by tender (entering on the flood tide) and there are some drying moorings in the river.

The river channel leads up to the village with old quay walls on the left

Facilities

There is a pub and a village stores/post office in the village square. Also a B&B on the main road.

More information

www.aberffraw.org

Comments

A new road bridge takes the coastal traffic to the north of the village so it is not blighted by traffic. The river is largely unspoilt and is a peaceful haven with only a few houses along the water's edge. The packhorse bridge forms part of the coast path and on the west side of the river the path follows the route of the river down to the sea from the village.

Bull Bay, Porth Llechog

The old quay wall which ships may have used to discharge their cargoes

The village of Bull Bay is probably best known for its golf course but also this most northerly village in Wales has a fascinating little harbour. It is perhaps ambitious to call this a harbour because the small cove is literally just that – a sheltered inlet that is well protected from the prevailing westerlies – but the rocky outcrops that litter the cove have been shaped to create two small inlets that provide a safe landing and a mooring place for boats in the summer.

This tiny cove was another of the places in Anglesey dedicated to shipbuilding, with the nearby woods providing a plentiful supply of the strong timbers required for the wooden ships of the day. The inlets in the cove were probably shaped to create a launching slipway for the ships. There is some evidence that Bull Bay was used for some of the exports of copper ore from the nearby Parys

Mountain site, but this would only have been likely if the facilities at nearby Amlwch were very busy so that Bull Bay provided an overflow facility.

Bull Bay also competed with Amlwch as a base for the small rowing pilot boats that would put out to service the shipping coming into Liverpool, and with pilotage in those days being a competitive business Bull Bay had the advantage of being closer to the incoming ships. However, once the pilots started using larger sailing cutters then Bull Bay lost out and the business focussed on Amlwch.

The cove would have been used by sailing ships coming in with cargoes such as coal, and farm produce and other cargoes would have been taken out. The sailing ships would have come in at high tide and landed their cargoes directly into horses and carts on the beach or alongside the small stone quay on the north side of the cove. There is an old lifeboat house at the head of the cove that closed around the turn of the 20th century.

Access by road

The A5025 coast road passes right above the cove and there is a signposted turning down to the cove. Postcode for SatNav is LL68 9SH.

One of the cleared channels between the rock outcrops that still provide boat moorings

Parking
Limited free parking along the sea front.

Water access
After rounding the headland into Bull Bay, Porth Llechog is immediately visible. There is anchorage off the cove in westerly winds and it is possible to land by tender. There is a launching fee payable for boat launching at Bull Bay.

Facilities
The Bull Bay Hotel overlooks the cove and there are limited facilities in the village.

More information
www.anglesey.gov.uk
Email pem@anglesey.gov.uk
☎ 01248 752300

Comments
In recent times there has been restoration work carried out along the sea wall and a new concrete slipway facilitates the launching of leisure craft. In the summer this is a popular place for launching small leisure craft and is particularly favoured by divers.

Amlwch

The history of the port of Amlwch is tied up very closely with the copper mines on Parys Mountain three miles inland. It has been suggested that copper was mined there in the Bronze Age and it is likely that the port was used to export the ore as far back as Roman times.

Amlwch starts as a tiny creek that widens into a deep cleft running in from the Irish Sea and it would have provided good shelter even without the modern breakwaters. When large-scale copper mining opened up around 1770 Amlwch was the logical port for the exports and its development started. Quays and jetties were built within the tight confines of the creek and you can still see the stone bins on the east side of the harbour where the ore would have been stored before being loaded into the sailing ships.

As the port developed there was a need for ship repairing which later developed into shipbuilding facilities, putting more pressure on the available space within the port where there is barely room to turn a ship round. To expand the port it is estimated that over 20,000 tons of rock were blasted out and piers were built to form the inner harbour much as it is seen today. It must have been exciting to sail into the narrow entrance between the piers and in rough weather the harbour entrance was closed off with baulks of timber. A watchhouse and an outer pier were built in 1816 but by the late 1880s much of the copper ore was being handled by the railways and the trade at the port declined. It received a boost in much more recent times when Amlwch was used as a marine terminal to service an offshore oil transshipment facility and new outer piers were built, along with boat pens for use by the service vessels and the pilot boats. Amlwch has a long association with the Liverpool Pilots and has served as a base for the pilot boats for many hundreds of years.

A fascinating feature of Amlwch is the dry dock, which was blasted out of the rock just outside the old port in the 19th century; it can still be seen but is

The pens for the pilot and service boats with the old dry dock cut into the rock on the right

no longer in use. Ships would be floated into the dock at high water, then a gate pulled across and the water drained out at low water. This dry dock is close by the new pilot and service boat pens and the breakwater which were built in 1976.

Access by road

From the A5025 take the turning to Amlwch at the roundabout and then follow the signs to the port. Postcode for SatNav is LL68 9HA.

Parking

A new free parking area with limited spaces has been created above the harbour close by the Liverpool Arms pub.

Water access

The entrance is simple between the new breakwaters once the entrance has been seen. The inner harbour dries and mooring there is alongside rough stone walls. It may be possible to find a temporary mooring in the pens but these are mainly occupied by fishing boats.

Facilities

There are three pubs near the parking area and full facilities in the town.

More information

www.anglesey.gov.uk
Maritime officer ☎ 01407 831065

Comments

Today there has been some restoration work in the port surroundings to make them more attractive to visitors and to maintain the history of this historical harbour. The inner harbour is now mainly used by local fishing boats and they, along with the pilot boats, also use some of the berths in the outer pens now that the oil terminal has closed down.

The convoluted old harbour now used mainly by fishing boats

Red Wharf Bay, Pentraeth

If you look at Red Wharf Bay at low tide it is difficult to imagine any ship or boating activity taking place here, but when the tide rises the bay is transformed into a wide expanse of water. The harbour area (what was the original Red Wharf) is on the northern side of the bay where the river channel winds its way out to sea and creates an access for boats at high tide.

The attraction of Red Wharf Bay in the past was its sheltered position with excellent protection from the prevailing westerlies and this, combined with a ready supply of timber from the surrounding woods, was what made this small port an important shipbuilding centre. Here many of the wooden sailing ships that were used to carry the copper ore from the Anglesey mines were built. The quay was also used to bring in cargoes – mainly coal from along the coast for local use, but a number of foreign vessels also came to the port with cargoes and there were exports of local stone and grain. The importance of the coal imports can be seen by the fact that there were four coalyards on the quay at one time. There are records of trading at the port

dating back to the 15th century, but it was the advent of steam ships, both bigger and more capable than the sailing ships, that killed off the trade and the shipbuilding at the port and today there are only a few reminders of the past.

Sailing boats still come to Red Wharf but these are yachts which are capable of drying out at their moorings. The formation of the port is interesting, with a spit of land sticking out parallel with the shore to offer shelter when the wind does turn to the east, and in addition to yachts there are a few local fishing boats. The name Red Wharf is reputed to come from the blood that flowed in a Viking battle that took place in 1170. The pub adjacent to the quay dates back to the 17th century and is one of the main reasons to visit Red Wharf today.

Access by road

The A5025 from Menai Bridge passes close, then watch out for the sign for a left turn to Red Wharf Bay. Postcode for SatNav is LL75 8RJ.

The attractive Ship Inn that looks out over the bay

Parking

Limited free parking on the quay and outside the pub.

Water access

Head for the distinctive headland close by the entrance and then pick up the buoyed channel to head in towards the quay. The buoys are laid by the local sailing club and are a summer-only feature. There are moorings in the harbour – these are private but there may be vacancies. Landing is by tender.

Facilities

Red Wharf Bay has excellent facilities in terms of cafés, restaurants and the pub. The Ship Inn is renowned for its food and this alone makes a visit worthwhile.

More information

Traeth Coch Sailing Club ☏ 01248 853795
www.traethcochsailingclub.org
Ship Inn ☏ 01248 852568

Comments

Today there is a wonderful air of tranquillity about Red Wharf Bay so come here for the peace and quiet and the views, but not for any signs of its historical past.

The stone bank that offers some protection to the inner part of the harbour

Port Penrhyn

Penrhyn was a small harbour at the entrance to the River Cegin just east of Bangor (when it was known as Aber Cegin) and it was established to serve local requirements, with quays on either bank of the river entrance.

Records dating back to 1713 show that the port handled the export of slates from the quarries at Bethesda as well as imports of coal and other goods. As the slate quarries were developed to become the largest in the world the port also expanded and became know as Port Penrhyn, as part of the Penrhyn Estates. With the slate being exported to both Ireland and the Continent, considerable development of the port took place, with a stone finger pier first being built out from the old port in 1790 then further extended in 1830.

Further expansion took the form of a second pier extending out further to the east to create a new enclosed dock basin, which made Port Penrhyn one of the largest ports along this coast. The magnificent dock office building with a gold clock that still remains demonstrates the importance of the port. The slates were brought down from the quarry on a railway line laid for the purpose and the track of this can still be seen but it has now been converted into a footpath. However, much remains of this important slate port and the value of the slate trade can be judged by the magnificent castle that the quarry owners had built alongside the port.

Port Penrhyn is still an active dock and you can get a great sense of what it must have been like in the past with all the slate export activity. Today there is a major mussel processing plant to handle the mussels dredged up at Conway and in the Menai Strait and gravel is distributed from a base at the pier head. There is a considerable yacht storage and sales area operated by Dickies. Whilst the main dock basin dries out at low water there are plans for dredging the entrance channel to encourage development of the dock and the large enclosed basin offers the possibility of a marina.

The clock on the harbour offices

Access by road
From the main A55 road turn off the signposted road to Bangor on the A5. There are signs to Port Penrhyn on the right-hand side after about three miles and several roundabouts. Postcode for SatNav is LL57 4HN.

Parking
Limited free parking inside the dock area.

Water access
Direct access from the eastern end of the Menai Strait.

The early part of the harbour that was based on the river channel

Facilities

Excellent dock facilities, but for pubs, cafés and shops the nearest are in the town of Bangor.

More information

Port Penrhyn Dock Office ☎ 01248 352525
www.port-penrhyn.co.uk
Dickies *Email* harbourmaster@portpenrhyn.co.uk
Email bangor@dickies.co.uk

Comments

You can get a considerable sense of history at Port Penrhyn, with the older buildings and the quays and still enough maritime activity to keep this an active port. Here is a port in transition rather than in decline.

Old crane located in the newer part of the dock that is still active

Rhos-on-Sea

Located between the major holiday resorts of Llandudno and Colwyn Bay and virtually a suburb of Colwyn Bay, Rhos-on-Sea is also a holiday resort but it has a small harbour too.

Whilst nearly all the harbours in Wales have long historical origins based on commercial activity and cargo handling, the harbour at Rhos-on-Sea was not developed as a harbour. The seas around Rhos have a long history as a prolific fishery area, with the fishery being originally developed by the monks from the nearby abbey. They built a fish weir in the waters off Rhos that would funnel the passing fish shoals into a net; this was in use up until the early 20th century and it is thought that it may have been the origin of the present harbour, although what is now the current harbour was only developed in the 1980s as part of a flood protection scheme.

The sea wall along the coast here is quite low and in storms there was a serious risk of the waves over-topping the wall and flooding the properties along the sea road. The rubble stone wall that was built some 300 yards offshore was designed to break up the force of the waves before they arrived on the beach. There was some surplus stone from the construction of the stone wall and this was used to

extend the groin that runs out from the point, which explains why the result was a harbour-shaped construction with an opening at its northern end. The construction is somewhat reminiscent of what the wooden-staked fish weir might have been like, with the gap at one end of about 50 yards, but this is purely coincidental – as was the use of the water inside the stone wall as a harbour.

Today it provides shelter for a small fleet of sea angling boats. The harbour dries out at low water and has to be dredged every few years to maintain a reasonable depth of water. There are plans to revitalise the area if funds can be found but it is not clear what work would be done on the harbour.

Access by road

Head into the town of Rhos-on-Sea and the harbour lies off the promenade at its northern end. Postcode for SatNav is LL28 4EP.

The rebuilt stone breakwater was established as a coast protection scheme and now creates a harbour

Dinghies stored along the sea front

Parking

Parking on the sea front.

Water access

Take a wide sweep around Rhos Point where a buoy marks a wreck. The harbour is best approached at the southern end of the breakwater but beware of a submerged section off the end and a partially submerged jetty extending out from the shore, both of which are marked by beacons. The harbour is full of allocated mooring buoys. It is best to anchor off in settled weather and there is a slipway on the shore adjacent to the remains of an old pier for tender landing.

Facilities

All the facilities of a small town, with pubs and cafés along the promenade.

More information

www.conwy.gov.uk/harboursandseaboard
Principal Harbour and Maritime Officer Conway Council ☎ 01492 596253

Comments

Rhos-on-Sea is the only harbour known to have been built by accident, but the fleet of fishing boats using this 'harbour' add interest to the seaside ambiance of Rhos-on-Sea and help to bring the place to life.

The tide pours over the half-tide wall at the northern end of the harbour

Foryd Harbour, Rhyl

Rhyl is best known as a holiday resort but the River Clwyd flowing out to sea to the west of the town has been a port for hundreds of years, possibly even back to Roman times.

For years the actual port was inland at Rhuddlan but as the river silted up the port moved downriver closer to the sea. By the 19th century a quay for coastal vessels had been built near the river mouth, the main cargo handled at the port being timber. The quay on the west side, close to where the modern bridge now crosses the river, was the general cargo landing quay, whilst on the east side of the harbour landing stages were built to create a terminus for passenger vessels bringing holidaymakers from Liverpool. It was this passenger trade that started Rhyl on the path to becoming an important holiday resort as it was the nearest resort to Liverpool and so a very popular place for a trip by paddle-steamer across from the River Mersey.

On the west side of the harbour coal from the Point of Ayr colliery was exported as some of the closer ports to the colliery on the Dee Estuary silted up. What used to be the coal quay has now been converted to serve the fleet of sea angling boats that operate from the harbour.

In recent years a large amount of money has been spent on developing this seaward section of the quay to create a base for these boats and in addition to the

quay area and its floating pontoon there is a large boat park behind the quay. The yacht club is based at the old section of the quay closer to the bridge and there are two slipways here. It is possible to explore the river above the Blue Bridge by tender and much of both the inner and outer sections of the harbour have been redeveloped, so much of the past history of Foryd harbour has been destroyed but there is still enough to get a feel for what this busy harbour might have looked like 100 years ago.

There is a wind farm established offshore from Rhyl and there are plans to expand the harbour so that it can serve as a base for the vessels serving this wind farm.

Access by road

The main A548 coast road passes over the harbour on the distinctive Blue Bridge, with a turning off to the harbour on the west side. Postcode for SatNav is LL18 5AR.

Parking

Limited free parking on the new sea angling quay. Pay and display parking on the east side of the Blue Bridge.

The remains of the old quay wall

Water access

The entrance channel is marked by beacons which should all be left on the port side going in. Entrance is possible after about half tide and there is temporary berthing alongside the yacht club quay, but this dries out. The mooring buoys in the harbour are fully allocated but the yacht club may be able to make a mooring available. The pontoon at the sea angling quay is only available for those boats.

Facilities

There is a pub and café close by the quay and the yacht club is open to visiting yachtsmen. Full facilities in the nearby town.

More information

www.rhylyachtclub.co.uk
① 01745 570 105

Comments

Like most seaside towns Rhyl is trying to reinvent itself to cater for the modern holidaymaker and a lot of money has been spent on upgrading the harbour to make it a centre for sea angling boats. The history of the harbour has not been considered in this upgrading, but it is still a busy and interesting harbour to visit and it contrasts with the holiday end of the town to the east.

An old wooden mooring post on the beach in the outer section of the harbour

The modern pontoon that provide facilities for the sea angling fleet

Greenfield Dock

Greenfield Dock is a small inlet off the Dee Estuary formed by a small river mouth, one of several small creeks in the area that connect up with the Dee Estuary. Greenfield Dock was probably in use centuries ago as a small port to serve the nearby abbey, but its main development as a dock stems from the 18th century when a copper works was developed to exploit the copper deposits from Anglesey. The raw copper was imported into Greenfield, where it was then processed into sheets (used for covering ship's bottoms to prevent the timbers deteriorating and for the manufacture of other goods). Greenfield ships traded mainly with Liverpool and in the 19th century a passenger trade was also established to transport pilgrims visiting nearby Holywell.

The port was unique along this coast in having a sluicing basin formed on the river above the actual port area, which would be filled on the rising tide and with the water coming down the river. This trapped water was then released at the next low water to flush away the mud that accumulated in the harbour.

At its peak in the 19th century there were cranes on the quays and a breakwater extending out into the estuary. Some of the old port facilities can still be seen, with part of the old quay wall and the sluicing pond still visible but neither is in use today (although the remains of the old sluice can still be seen under the road bridge). What used to be the breakwater running out into the estuary is now a slipway where it is possible to launch and recover boats.

Despite the restoration work that has been carried out around the harbour there is an air of decay about Greenfield Dock and it is a long way from its former glory as a busy harbour.

Access by road

From the A584 coast road turn towards the sea at Greenfield along Dock Road.

Parking

Free car parking on both sides of the harbour.

Water access

Straight in from the estuary channels, but there are no facilities in the harbour and nowhere to moor. Beware of ropes running right across the dock in many places. It is possible to land by tender on the slipway on the east side of the entrance from half tide onwards.

Facilities

The village facilities in Greenfield are a short walk from the harbour.

More information

www.greenfielddocks.co.uk

Comments

The area around the dock has been tidied up and gentrified to make it a tourist attraction with parking and railings but the dock itself is filled with mud and is home to a rather sad collection of boats, most of which look as though they will never go to sea again. On the east side of the dock is a waste disposal plant and to the west there is a sewage farm but you can still get a good sense of the history of the place.

The partially restored dock is filled with many boats that will never go to sea again

Flint

This inlet from the Dee Estuary is little more than a muddy creek today, but it rose to fame as a port when the Muspratt & Huntley chemical factory in Liverpool was forced out of that metropolis because of the obnoxious fumes it created. However, the original port at Flint was located on the moat that surrounded Flint Castle, with separate quays here for the town and the castle. This castle harbour and the moat are now fully silted up but their location can still be seen around the castle ruins.

The industrial quay was developed in the creek further seaward and before the chemical works was established this creek at Flint had previously been a small port serving the local communities. Now it was used to import the raw materials and export the

The channel leading into the dock is now silted up to a large degree

finished products of the chemical factory. Other industries followed the chemical plant and the Port of Flint and its surroundings were a hive of activity in the late 19th and early 20th centuries. Lead, timber and coal were the main cargoes handled and a shipyard was also established. However, the chemical factory was still spewing out pollutants and it was closed down around 1900, which started the decline of the harbour. Chemicals came back to Flint when Courtaulds established a major factory there after the Second World War, but this factory used the railways for its raw materials and finished goods so the harbour fell into disuse. That plant followed its predecessor and is now closed, and the area surrounding the creek has now been developed as a large industrial estate with everything going in and out by road.

Further south there are the remains of the very imposing castle where the old port was located and the line of the moat can still be traced. With both the castle moat and the creek as seen today it is hard to picture them as busy ports in the past and this is one of the places where leisure craft have not taken over from the commercial use.

Access by road

From the A548 turn seawards over the railway, following the signs to the castle. From here follow the road west through the industrial estate to the creek. Postcode for SatNav is CH6 5PE.

Parking

On road alongside the harbour and in a car park near the castle.

Water access

Follow the main channel up the Dee Estuary and the creek at Flint lies just around Flint Point. There are strong currents across the entrance and access is only about two hours either side of high water. There is nowhere to tie up in the creek, although part of the old quay remains at the head of the creek.

Facilities

All the facilities of a small town are available in Flint.

More information

North Wales Tourism www.nwt.co.uk

Comments

Some improvement to the road access around the creek has been carried out in an attempt to smarten up the area and it is possible to walk right out to Flint Point and to follow a coast path here. Part of the old quay wall is still visible at the top end of the creek but today the creek lies in peace and there is a very sudden transformation from the busy industrial estate to the peace and quiet of the estuary waters. Best visited at high water when the extensive mud of the creek disappears.

The castle where the moat formed a harbour serving the castle and the town

A derelict boat disappearing into the silt

Connah's Quay

Chester was a major port back in Roman times and the centre for trade over a large area. However, the River Dee that leads up to Chester from the Irish Sea gradually silted up over the years and this, combined with the use of larger ships, made Chester inaccessible except for small barges.

The River Dee New Cut was built in 1737 to bypass a section of the silted river and it was the building of this New Cut that created the quay at Connah's Quay. The area here is rich in minerals (mainly coal and iron ore) and in addition to their use in local smelters these minerals from the local mines were shipped out to Ireland, France and Spain. In time Connah's Quay became a place of transshipment for inbound cargoes and for the export of coal from the nearby coalfields, and it owes its existence to the availability of good water depths in the channel in from the Dee Estuary.

Unlike many ports Connah's Quay survived the coming of the railway in the mid-19th century because of its transshipment trade and indeed the building of the railway brought additional cargoes to the port for export. However, silting has always been a major problem in the River Dee and its

The modern quay was is now home to a motley collection of small boats

estuary and just as Connah's Quay benefitted from the silting further upriver so other ports further out in the estuary benefitted from the silting at Connah's Quay and the trade moved to ports further seaward.

The old wooden quay fell into disrepair and about 30 years ago the old quay was rebuilt. The new quay wall was a substantial concrete structure that lines the river and it is mainly used by fishing boats and craft being refitted.

In addition to the main quay Connah's Quay also has small deck basins built into the river bank and one remains. This old dock lies downstream from the main quay as a silted inlet outside the Old Quay House pub. This dock basin was probably one of the old shipyards and it gives a flavour of what the port was like centuries ago. The name Connah is reputed to come from a one-time landlord of the Old Quay House pub.

Access by road

From the A584 main coast road turn under or over the railway close by the railway station and the road leads on to the quay. Postcode for SatNav is CH5 4DS.

The silted dock basin that was once home to a shipyard. The Old Quay House is in the centre

Parking

Free parking on the quay and outside the pub.

Water access

Follow the buoyed channel through the Dee Estuary, with Connah's Quay located where the estuary turns into the river channel. Mooring is available alongside the rebuilt quay but there is a considerable rise and fall of tide here and the quay wall is not very yacht-friendly.

Facilities

All the usual facilities of a small town are just a walk away from the quay. There is the Old Quay House pub at the old dock area close by the quay.

More information

Connah's Quay Town Council
www.connahs-quay.co.uk
Clwyd-Powys Archaeological Trust
www.cpat.org.uk

Comments

With the steelworks across the river and a nearby power station this is not the prettiest of dock areas, but these features do reflect the industrial past of the area. The dock basin is full of derelict-looking craft that will probably never go to sea again and there is a similar air about the whole place despite the creation of riverside walks.